I'LL TAKE SPAGHETTI BUT HOLD THE MAYO!

GREG HENDERSON

Greg Henderson

FAITH · SPORTS · BUSINESS · HUMOR · LIFE

QUADS
MEDIA
FIRM

This book is a work of fiction. Any references to historical events, real people, or real places are used fictitiously. Other names, characters, places, and events are products of the author's imagination, and any resemblance to actual events or places or persons, living or dead, is entirely coincidental.

Because of the dynamic nature of the Internet, any web addresses or links contained in this book may have changed since publication and may no longer be valid. The views expressed in this work are solely those of the author and do not necessarily reflect the views of the publisher, and the publisher hereby disclaims any responsibility for them.

"I'll Take Spaghetti but Hold the Mayo!"

Paperback: ISBN   978-1-959533-49-8

Library of Congress Control Number: 2023903364

All materials used for this book was from the Author

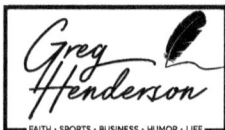

FAITH · SPORTS · BUSINESS · HUMOR · LIFE

TABLE OF CONTENTS

DEDICATION

I write this for my grandson Gamble and his soon to be born sister. I wanted these stories to be told and remembered for you and your future generations. I also dedicate this to my wife Kathy. We have had an amazing and wonderful journey so far. I hope the Lord blesses us with many more awesome years, but if He for some reason chooses another option Kathy, I will see you on the other side!

PROLOGUE

Thank you, Albertville.

Kathy and I were having dinner with our good friends Mark and Lesa Davis a few weeks prior to this writing. Our discussion turned to our town and in particular my loyalty and love for it. We talked about high school and my volunteer work with the tennis and basketball programs. We all graduated from Albertville. Lesa currently works for the school system and Kathy did for thirteen years. Mark played football, ran track and was crowned king of AHS. The Davis' children and ours also graduated from Albertville and were involved with many activities. Mark made a statement and asked me a question, "We all love Albertville and Albertville High School, but what drives you to work so hard for the teams and volunteer the hours that you do?" My answer was, "I can only tell you this. I loved entering the basketball games in high school and the response of the crowd when I would give it my all. When I was playing tennis and beginning to play well, there were so many people in town that encouraged and supported me. Day after day, I would hear people ask about my game, where was my next tournament, how did you do in the latest rankings and then they would encourage me and tell me to go win. So, I began to imagine when I was playing in tournaments that my whole town was in the stands. I began to play the best I could and give it my all. I had to help make the people and my fellow Aggies proud. Their encouragement pushed me to want to succeed so bad that I just could not give in. Their words helped me get a college tennis scholarship and pay for my education while enabling me to see parts of the country that I would not have otherwise. So that is it. I want to give back. I want the Aggies to be a success in everything. I believe Albertville is worthy of the best. It makes me happy to help young people achieve things that they did not know they could accomplish." So thank you to all in my hometown that helped me accomplish my dreams. There are a lot of you. I hope you know who you are.

AN AGGIE IN VEGAS

I am about to type two words that will scare some of you reading this book into closing this book, burning this book or throwing this book about as far as I do a sandwich ruined with the application of mayonnaise. The two words happen to describe the culture of which I am a part and in which I was raised. Here we go. The words are southern and Christian. The rest of the country does not always understand Southerners. This can lead to many interesting misconceptions about our part of the world. I got my college degree from the University of Nevada, Las Vegas. How I got there is a story for another day. In my days of roaming across the campus, I was given the nickname of Bama. That is all anyone knew to call me. It was not a hard nickname to get. All I really had to do is show up with a southern accent from the state of Alabama. The good and bad part of that is when someone mentioned Bama, everyone knew who was being talked about. One of the aforementioned misconceptions came from a classmate from New York City named Kirk Posmantur.

He had been a fan of the television show The Dukes of Hazard. I really think he was a fan of Catherine Bach and her famous Daisy Dukes, but I gave him the benefit of the doubt. Kirk was shocked to hear that there were paved roads and almost fell to the ground when I mentioned interstates. He thought it was all dirt roads, backwoods, and beautiful girls. He was mostly right. There were and still are some dirt roads, but they are not that prevalent. There were and still are a lot of backwoods. Certainly, there were and still, are a lot of beautiful southern girls. After learning of his affection for The Dukes of Hazzard I was just glad to be known as Bama and not Cooter. That would have made for a bad couple of years. So we did have paved roads, but Marshall County where I was from was a dry county. My intrigued UNLV classmates naturally assumed that I meant that it did not rain much. When I explained that the term dry county meant that alcohol could not be sold in any stores or served in any restaurant, they could not believe it. "Why would anyone want to live there?" I heard that question quite often. I argued the point that it was not a bad thing and that folks just drove about eight miles, crossed the county line and bought whatever they wanted. It would be another twenty plus years before my hometown would vote to sell alcohol. This happened when a law

14

passed allowing cities in dry counties to vote their own conscience.

As I grew up in Alabama, I learned from my grandparent's front porch in the Omaha community of Randolph County that when a car passed you stopped what you were doing and either gave them a good nod of the head if your hands were busy shelling peas or better yet you waved. A car would go by and I would ask, "Who was that, granddaddy?" He knew most of the folks in the area and he would tell me their name. Every once in a while, someone would drive by that he did not know. This did not matter. He still waved. Fifty years later it is still that way in small-town Alabama. Folks are just friendly and if you drive by you should expect a wave or an acknowledgment. If you do not wave back it is considered rude and you should then expect a different kind of acknowledgment from the initiator. If you are new to the area you get a pass for a few days as people will begin a conversation with you with the words "you ain't from around here now, are ya?" I never understood why the word now is used in those situations, but it just is.

If you happen to be walking by someone on the street of a small town in the Deep South you do not have to wave, but you do have to nod your head and acknowledge the other person. Usually, this is a greeting similar to "How you doing?" Now, unless it is a friend, you don't stop or wait for an answer. It is not meant to start a conversation. It is meant to say, hey, I acknowledge your existence as a human being and I have no ill will or reason to dislike you. We in the south like this. If someone on the street does not acknowledge you with a greeting, then that person is automatically regarded as someone that cannot be trusted and "we'll just keep an eye on them" is a phrase usually associated with the non-communicator.

This brings us back to the campus in Las Vegas. The young Southern Christian, me, had just left the student union building after registering for classes. While in the student union, God showed out as only He can do. I had not yet met anyone at UNLV and I was a little overwhelmed moving to the place known as "Sin City" to study. As a Christian, I was concerned about finding someone that shared my beliefs. As I was concluding the registration process, I looked across the lobby of the building. A young man was walking toward me.

His name was Hollis Kim. He had grown up in Hawaii and now worked with Intervarsity Fellowship, a Christian organization on campus. We had a great talk. I shared my faith with him and immediately knew that I had someone that I could talk with if a future need presented itself. This was an amazing faith strengthening moment in my Christian life. I had always heard that God was everywhere and the verse from Matthew 28:20 of the Bible, "and surely I am with you always even until the very end of the world," but I got to experience it first hand. Imagine that God cared enough about me to send a Christian to be the very first person I met in Las Vegas. That encouraged me as a believer and I never looked back. I went to my apartment and looked in the phone book (remember those things) for a church to attend. I found the First Southern Baptist Church of Las Vegas and I would attend there during my time in the community.

The campus at UNLV had several buildings spread over the desert landscape. Each had a sidewalk leading to the front door. On the sidewalk were large footprints and each building had a different color of footprint leading to it. The science building might have green feet, the business building would be blue, and footprints leading to the athletic department were, of course, the school colors of scarlet and gray. I am not sure what color led to the library and I am not sure what that says about my study habits. As classes started and I followed the colored footprints on the sidewalk to the desired destination, I started my quest to spread the "salt and light" talked about in Matthew 5:13-14 also in the Bible. I would pass another student, nod and say, "how ya doin'?" You would not think that with one hundred degree days in the desert that it would take very long to melt ice. It seemed like from the cold shoulders and crazy stares I was receiving from my fellow students that I would never be able to penetrate their frigid personas. Finally, after about three weeks of tracing the same route and seeing the same people while following the properly colored feet, greeting them with the same greeting while looking them in the eye, a guy looked back and said "hey." Finally, contact. It was as if I was in a sci-fi film playing the part of an astronaut that had finally communicated with the newly discovered civilization. I was now determined to keep it up. Actually, it worked pretty well. The one person communicating turned into many others as we all became accustomed to our daily routines. Before long we were chatting in the student union, playing ping-pong, or trying to get a quick bite from the cafeteria. They were not deep friendships. As a matter-of-fact, I doubt anyone knew my real name. But for me, Bama was just fine. I think it actually made it easier for them to be courteous to me. I was the UNLV version of a foreign exchange student only from the south.

Actually, I did wind up with a couple of good friends. Steve Tallent of Washington and Tom Kieley of Colorado. We had similar interest and neither of us was into the partying scene. We would meet at the cafeteria on Saturday mornings for brunch. After a couple of weeks, the servers knew me and immediately cut my biscuit in two halves for me and then added the gravy on top. One particular Saturday I fooled everyone when I held up my hand on the biscuit and gravy and mentioned that I was going to get a pastry at the end of the counter. I got the eggs, bacon and went for one of the hot and fresh looking donuts. After Tom, Steve and I were seated, I took a big bite of the donut. Boy was I disappointed. I was hoping for the sweet tasting, sugar or cinnamon-coated, creamed filled treat. Instead, my mouth was filled with a plain, bland and bread-like bite. "Aw! That is the worst donut I have ever tasted." Steve and Tom looked at each other looked at me, back at each other and started laughing. Steve finally composed himself enough to say, "You mean to tell me that you have never had a bagel." I responded. "I have never even heard of a bagel. Why is it disguised as a donut and why would anyone ever eat one?" The guys then proceeded to tell me of all the crazy things people put on bagels. I could not understand why anyone would place cream cheese and locks (which I later found out was fish) on breakfast bread. It was after all 1980 and bagels were not on the menu at most southern breakfast restaurants, much less served in the homes. So many laughed at the kid from Alabama that did not know everything about breakfast cuisine. After the chuckle, I challenged anyone within earshot to a grit eating contest. I got no takers; of course, the cafeteria did not have grits anyway.

When I moved back to Alabama after graduation, I lost track of my two friends although I have a story about each. UNLV had one of the best Hotel Administration programs in the world and still does. Tom graduated in hotel management and had a job at one of the famous hotels on the Las Vegas strip. He was working at the front desk one evening when a couple checked in from Albertville. He looked at the registration and said, "I noticed you are from Albertville. Would you happen to know Greg Henderson?" He explained our connection and friendship. The folks from back home thought that was the most amazing thing and went back to Albertville telling folks how everyone in Las Vegas seemed to know Greg. I tried to explain that almost all UNLV students worked at the hotels and it was just a coincidence, but people tend to like the intrigue, so after a while, I just went with it. I still see those people from time to time and they always smile and bring up Tom and their encounter.

Steve's was a different situation. It would be thirty-one years before I heard from Steve. Then one day out of the blue, my phone rings and it is like I am standing next to him again. I recognized his voice immediately. Steve has always been and still is a Washington State Cougar sports fan and it just so happened on August 31, 2013, the Cougars were scheduled to play a game at Auburn University in Auburn, Alabama. Steve had always wanted to visit a Southeastern Conference stadium for a football game so he got game tickets and airline tickets for him and his wife Kristi. He was coming to Alabama and hoping to get together for dinner with Kathy and I. He had his trip planned and knew exactly where he wanted to eat. He chose Big Bob Gibson's Barbeque in Decatur. He would fly into Birmingham on Friday, rent a car and drive up I65 to Decatur. Now Alabama has numerous, numerous barbeque places. Many of them are very good. As a matter of fact, Kathy and I would be driving about sixty miles and pass a few of the really good joints on the way. Steve and Kristi would be driving ninety miles and passing by my personal favorite Ken's barbeque in Birmingham to get to Big Bob Gibson's. I took a moment to mention that Kathy and I would gladly drive to Birmingham and meet them so that they would not have to drive that distance each way. Steve insisted. It seems that he had studied up on things to try in Alabama and apparently Big Bob Gibson's was a must experience. At this time, I had lived in Alabama most of my fifty-three years and had never experienced this particular barbeque. Steve was traveling across the country and if that is where he wanted to eat, then that is where we would eat. The food was very good, but the reunion and fellowship were even better. The next night Steve got to experience a great atmosphere at Jordan-Hare Stadium as his Cougars took Auburn to the wire before losing 31-24. He had a blast.

A couple of my college professors had their own opinions about the South and Alabama. In my first year at UNLV, my marketing professor told stories of his short teaching stint at Auburn University. He shared how he could not understand people in the south and the culture surrounding Auburn. Needless to say, it was just not his style. It seemed he could not start his daily classes without saying

22

something derogatory about country music, the one horse college town, sweet tea or the evangelical efforts of the southern believers. The professor had no idea I was from Alabama. Most people with a southern accent attending UNLV were from no further away than Texas, and that was rare. I devised a plan and called my good friend Joe Alldredge. Joe and I had grown up only a few houses apart in good ole Albertville. He was now attending the verbally maligned "cow college." I gave him a call and asked for a favor. A couple of weeks later I entered the class wearing a bright orange t-shirt with navy blue lettering that had "AUBURN" in bold letters and beneath it in smaller letters, "the University of Alabama." My professor looked at me and then looked at my shirt. His jaw started to drop and a little bead of sweat began to appear around his temple.

Now, Albertville is in north Alabama and Auburn is about three and a half hours away very close to the Georgia line in the central part of the state. I had anticipated what might transpire in a conversation and decided to turn up the heat on the professor. He did indeed follow the planned script that I had projected and asked, "Are you from Alabama?" I answered that I was. "What part?" This is where I lied. First I did not think he would know where Albertville was and second I wanted him to squirm a bit. I had thought about what to say and did not want to say I was from Auburn. It would seem too obvious. I thought of a town close to Auburn. If someone had lived in Auburn, they would have certainly heard of the town. If they were not from that part of the state, they would not have heard of the town. "Opelika." His head dropped as the name of Auburn's border town hit his ears. He started backpedaling on all the things he had said. The professor suddenly really liked his time there and thought the people were great. The town was a little small for his liking, but the University had a lot going for it. For me, this was a great moment. The derogatory jokes died down a bit although he still mentioned his time in the south. A couple of weeks after the t-shirt revenge, I let him off the hook and told him I was actually from Albertville. I was right. He had never heard of it. We had a good laugh and developed a good student/professor relationship. I even made a good grade without having to find out what color the footprints were that led to the library. My professor also had a new first day of class routine. He began by asking, "Is anybody from Alabama?"

During my business communications class in my senior year at

UNLV, I had a different professor that also did not think much of the education of the adults in the Deep South. By this time, most of my fellow students knew that the person they called Bama was from Alabama. I sat listening intently to the ongoing lecture surrounded by a couple of my teammates from the Rebel tennis squad. The professor during his explanation of excellent business letter writing mentioned that as students we must remember to try to write our letters on no more than an eighth-grade level. He went on to explain that if you were writing letters to someone in the south like Alabama, only about 5% of the people in the state graduated from high school. It was instantaneous euphoria as my arms reached high in the sky and the cheers started. The professor did not understand the ruckus and asked for a little restraint. Someone quickly explained that the guy in the corner with the victory smile was from Alabama. The professor began to apologize, but I quickly stopped him. "No sir, don't apologize. You actually confirmed that I was in the top 5%. I have been trying to tell these guys they were in the company of greatness." After a few jeers and a lot of laughter, the professor went back to the lecture, a little confused and not sure what to do next. I thought for sure after that I would do well in the class. A couple of weeks later he handed me a graded business letter with red writing. I just read it and shook my head as he strolled by semi-laughing to himself. Curious classmates looked my way. The laughter started when I turned my paper around and they viewed, "Good work Bama, but not in my top 5%." At least he knew who I was, or at least my nickname.

THE BEST-LAID SCHEMES "O' MICE AN' MEN"

It is amazing that for 242 years those words have reverberated time and time again through the minds of people from countries all over the world. The title of this chapter is an excerpt from the poem To a Mouse, originally written by the famous Scotsman Robert Burns. Robert apparently was inspired after destroying the nest of a field mouse while ploughing, causing the family of mice to scurry about, leaving the home they desperately needed to survive the harsh winter. At this point, you are thinking, "what in the world is ploughing?" I know I was. In the United States and Canada, we use the correct term of plowing. Why do I know it is correct, you ask? Simple, because we use it and we are Americans. Apparently, the European, English speaking nations still prefer ploughing and ole Robert was one of them.

So, what does any of that have to do with the Beam family? Plenty and it has to do with, you guessed it, Mr. Beam's favorite son-in-law, Joey. As a matter of fact, this story begins with the days of our youth in good old Albertville, Alabama. Joey is older than me by almost three months, but due to the small age difference, we were in the same grade in school and played sports in the same youth league age groups. It is hard to remember the first time I met Joey. We just kind of knew each other, probably through sports as we played against each other. I imagine it started with neighborhood choose-up games. Joey grew up on some acreage and close to a creek just outside of town. He learned how to shoot a gun and he worked hard with farm-like chores. I grew up in town on a small lot and my work consisted of taking out the trash and occasionally mowing the yard. As adults, Kathy and I would raise our family in a home with a few acres on a creek and Joey would reside with his tribe in a home on a small lot in the city. I am not sure what that means, but it is interesting. My days as a youth were spent mostly at "Johnson's Stadium", the local vacant lot owned by Mr. L. P. Johnson, who also owned the local Piggly Wiggly grocery. We used that property as our very own sandlot.

I remember one Little League baseball evening when we were ten, maybe eleven years old. I played for a team sponsored by Bryant

Manufacturing, a company that made furniture in our hometown. Joey played for the Civitans, the local chapter of the civic club that started almost 100 years ago in Birmingham, Alabama. Many other businesses in town took part with sponsorships and I vowed then that I would do the same thing in the future if given the chance. I made good on that promise as our real estate firm sponsored a team for years. I also joined the Albertville Civitan club in 1987 and am still a member. If you do not think that your actions of kindness toward the youth have an effect on their future, then let me tell you from personal experience, it really does have an impact. The league had six teams and we played two games a week, one on Tuesday and the other on Friday. We always got there early to see all the games. This particular evening, Joey and I were walking around the park watching the other teams and enjoying time with another friend of ours and teammate of Joey, Larry Nelson. Joey had close-cut black hair, the typical style of a kid that age. I was sometimes sporting a flat top, especially in the summer months. Larry, well his hair had a natural curl to it and even at this young age, he was starting to grow what in high school would be his famous white man's afro. This would lead to a loving nickname of "Fro". But that would be a few years from now. At this point, we had just left Mr. Cannady,

Joey's dad and were strolling with our backs to him in our nice uniforms, me on the left, Joey in the middle and Larry on the right. Fran Tarkenton was a hero of mine growing up and every time that I could, I would wear the number ten as was the case that season. Larry wore number 12 for the Civitans and Joey number eleven. I have remembered for over 45 years what Mr. Cannady said as he was laughing. "Hey look, the three stooges, ten, eleven and twelve." I thought it was about the numbers and we laughed for a moment, then I thought more about it. Joey's dark hair could have resembled that of Mo. Larry with his hat on the Afro in the making could certainly be Larry. That left me, the guy with the flat top to be Curly. We were quite a sight.

I want to say a little more about Larry before moving on. He was one of those guys everyone liked. The girls loved his 'fro and dazzling smile. He had a sense of humor that was infectious. We spent many summer days riding bikes and visiting friends. We always remained good friends, but when the age of sixteen came along and Larry was able to date, life began to change. I watched in amazement as Larry with his charm, wit, and looks could get a date with any girl in school.

He would spend most of his spare time with some very nice looking young lady by his side. He even had the most famous collection in Albertville High School history. It seemed he was able to talk almost every girl that he went out with into giving him the label from her panties. Not only that, they would initial them for him. It was crazy. He kept them in his wallet and would impress all the guys with the latest prized ribbon.

Larry was also a good athlete. He continued to play baseball in high school for the Aggies but was best known for his ability to run cross-country. He would not however let cross-country interfere with his party life nor would the partying interfere with cross-country. Many Saturdays and Sundays you could find Larry at the track running, sweating and attempting to release the entire intake of the previous evening. He would do this so the coaches would not smell his sweat Monday at practice and know that he had been up to a little underage consumption. He was the top runner for the Aggies and one of the best in Marshall County. He told the story of the county championship cross-country meet like this. "Well Greg, I was leading after about two miles (of the 3.1-mile race). Then Louis Lusk (of Guntersville, a high school a few miles away) pulled alongside me. We ran together chatting away. We knew that we were both trying to figure out when to make our move. With about a quarter of a mile left, Louis said do you think anyone is close to us? I turned my head to check and when I did, he took off. I tried to run him down but could not, so I finished second." I felt bad for Larry, but he just laughed about it and said that he should have known better and just plain got snookered.

Larry would later use that speed in another way. He was the second most famous streaker in AHS history. Streaking was the 1970's fad of getting naked except for your sneakers and running through populated areas such as shopping malls, ball fields or someplace similar. There is no evidence to prove that the famous song "The Streak" by Ray Stevens has anything to do with Mrs. Beam looking for bacon at the meat counter when a streaking event occurred at the local Piggly Wiggly, or the fact that Ray's famous line "Don't look Ethel" was actually originally "Don't look Martha" as Mr. Beam was heard shouting to his wife from the jelly aisle.

The top honor for streaking in Albertville folklore still belongs to Tommy Winkles. This was way before everyone had a cell phone that could photograph or videotape anything and everything. It would be eyewitness accounts and word of mouth that would keep the story going until this date. The local myth had it that Tommy streaked on three different occasions and actually streaked in front of the police station window. That was indeed no more than folklore. The truth was even more impressive. Tommy actually made a streak through the middle of our crowded mall. We will use nicknames or aliases for his accomplices, but Tommy did have help. The driver referred to as Hutch slowly positioned the car with the passenger side close to the mall doors. This particular evening the mall was buzzing with activity as rumors had spread that a possible streak would take place. The line to the Baskin Robbins and the thirty-one flavors of ice cream created the first obstacle as Tommy studied from the car window his route around the patrons. The high school senior designated as the manager of the restaurant that evening, later mentioned that the store had record sales and had to restock several flavors, totally selling out of banana nut fudge.

Hutch could see the people beginning to point and look at the car. He encouraged that it was now or never. That was all Tommy needed as he leaped from the passenger door without a stitch of clothes on his body except a pair of purple converse tennis shoes. He had to slow for just a moment as he opened the mall door to start his full sprint down the mall. The middle of the mall featured the famous water fountain now surrounded by Albertville High School students pointing, screaming, laughing but not looking away from the sight. After passing the fountain, Tommy's mind was on the back door. At a comet-like pace, he could see the driver's of the getaway vehicle, Shep and Mo, as they pressed their faces against the glass of the rear doors to see Tommy's progress. He was zipping past Alleyway records hearing the Doobie

Brothers' song Takin' it to the Streets wafting into the mall from the music store. He somehow remembered the "no more need to worry" lyrics of the song for the rest of the evening and through the years. The whole ordeal took about ten seconds, but as Usain Bolt has shown us, the right ten seconds of a person's life can produce a legend. Shep and Mo had sprinted into position opening the car door for Tommy and sliding back to the driver's spot. Tommy went through the back doors of the mall and into the back seat and then they were gone from the mall. It is kind of ironic that the soon to come movie theaters were not yet built at the back of the mall, because Tommy was not through, not in the least. This night in

Albertville could have made for a great "B" movie like The Night of the Lepus or some such, but this would have been called The Night of the Streaker. Tommy was now on a mission to spread his charm everywhere.

He and his driver chose the local pool hall as the next target. Usually, the owner of the pool halls had a person charged with taking care of the building and making sure the patrons did not get overzealous. In the case of the pool hall downtown, the gentleman in charge had an interesting nickname. Years of life and a non-athletic frame had left the gentleman quite shy on the quickness scale, so of course, he was called Lightning. Tommy had played a few games at the hall over the years and after a game was over the famous reset command of "rack 'em, Lightning" would fill the air. Tommy was confident that he could speed past Lightning and escape. He took off. A plume of chalk dust permeated through the air as Tommy hit full stride past the slate and felt tables. He sure had no intention of slowing down as one of the players shouted, "Rack 'em" just before he reached the passenger door of the getaway car to escape.

The last place that would get to know Tommy very personally was the local burger and corndog place know as the Key Korner.

Fortunately, it was not a big building but it was a popular hangout in the community. After that, Tommy called it an evening. To this day no one in Albertville has topped the streaking trifecta of Tommy Winkles. Larry tried, as did a few others but to no avail. Yes, in Tommy's case, the fact was far better than folklore, although he later admitted the police station was not a bad idea.

Although Larry and Tommy were kindred spirits, their paths had not crossed much due to the age difference. That would change as they actually lived in an apartment together in their college days at Jacksonville State University. They were both dating Susan at the time, not the same Susan, but girls both named Susan. The two Susans were friends and so the guys had become friends. By the end of the fall semester, both found themselves without steady girls. Then one early spring day, the skies turned favorable and the temperatures reached high enough to beckon some of the coeds to the apartment pool to work on their tans. One such student caught the attention of both Tommy and Larry. In a moment they were by the pool tossing to the side their aerospace engineering studies. As Tommy would later explain, "we introduced ourselves to Janice, turned on all of our charms and she invited us to dinner that very evening. Of course, Larry wound up winning her heart and eventually the two were married." Larry and Janice had two daughters. We kidded him about that and how he was going to handle the male suitors when the girls became old enough to date. Life can throw some ironic twists in our direction. Larry also used his charm in sales at his work. He could land a job anywhere. He would take a job and be doing great, a customer would come in and talk with him and soon would offer him a position with a new company for more money. It seemed to happen on a regular basis.

I am getting ahead of myself and want to share one of their collegiate stories. This story involving Larry and Tommy is legendary as well. Tommy had a behavioral psychology class that used experiments on pigeons. The subjects were kept in the biology lab. One experiment used a pigeon that was to be monitored for a time and then placed on a diet until it reached 80% of its beginning weight. The students would then see if they could entice the bird to do tricks for food. Tommy was in charge of making sure the pigeon was fed. One Friday, he forgot to feed the pigeon. Thinking of the situation late in the evening and well after the science building was locked for the weekend, he decided that he had to find a way into the building and take care of the bird. Of course Larry and two other cohorts that we will call Tim and Lee had to go to make sure everything went well. The quartet somehow managed to make their way into the science building, then into the biology lab and fed the bird. As they were leaving they noticed two skeletons that they decided appeared lonely and also underfed. Then, being the good-hearted guys that they were, decided to take the bones home and offer them companionship. Amazingly they made it all the way to the apartment complex without detection. Now came the trick of getting them in without causing a scene. Tim decided to put a coat on one of the human frames then placed his arm around it as he would an evening date. Lee walked the other one doubled over as he would a friend that had overindulged during the evening.

The skeletons stayed with them for some time as a campus-wide search for the bony structures became more and more aggressive. Finally, someone ratted them out. The police came and found the skeletons at the apartment. Folklore had one of them at a table with playing cards in his fingers and poker chips stacked in front of him. The foursome was all in quite a bit of trouble with the university.

Although the police were laughing as they whisked Tommy downtown along with the skeletons, it was a bit of a serious situation. It seems that the cost of the skeletons was over one thousand dollars, which constituted a felony. There were several interesting moments in the interrogation room. One of those moments featured the police questioning Tommy as he sat at one end of the table and a skeleton in a chair at the opposite side of the room. Tommy, beginning to realize the seriousness of the situation tried to maintain a composed posture, but soon the eyes begin to twinkle and the smile started and then a burst of laughter echoed in the room. The police were a bit surprised as they asked him what he thought was so funny. He pointed toward the work of art that was adorned with a New York Yankee hat, a woman's bra (we think Larry had something to do with obtaining that), a Blue Nun wine bottle in one hand, a Bud Light can in the other and a squashed cigarette butt in its mouth. The kicker for the attire was the pair of purple converse tennis shoes. These were the same shoes worn by Tommy in the infamous evening of streaking in Albertville. "Come on," Tommy encouraged while pointing at the masterpiece, "that is funny." The laughter heard down the hall from the interrogation room confirmed that even the police could not keep a straight face at the site and the whole situation. The felony charges were lowered but the university did ask Tommy and his entourage to find other schools to pursue their studies.

I had a chance to talk with Tommy years later and we talked about some of those moments. He mentioned that some of the old gang wanted him to pull a 45th-anniversary reenactment of the streak at the still standing mall in a couple of years. I understand the presales of purple converse tennis shoes are going well just on the rumor. I think Tommy is more worried about pulling a hammy at the planter that was formally the fountain. That would make for an interesting headline in the local newspaper, "Man in his sixties carted away in ambulance after streaking incident at local mall." Maybe he will do it, I certainly would not put it past him. I suppose time will tell. We talked at length about our good friend Larry and all the fun times we shared with him. We laughed for a while and then we cried as we tried to figure out why in the world Larry in his thirties took a stroll into the woods alone, only to be carried out with a sheet pulled over his head by two men and an escort of uniformed personnel. Tommy told me, "I loved that guy." I agreed and said, "I wish I could have been there, maybe I could have said something to get him to change his mind." "Me too", Tommy said, "me too."

From that night at the little league field and the years to come, Joey and I shared a lot of similar interests. We would at age fourteen, play for the same baseball team as I played shortstop and Joey third base. We considered it a challenge to keep the left fielder from touching a ball that stayed below ten feet in the air. I cringed one evening as a hotshot ball hit from an opposing player toward Joey at third, hit a hump in the field, took a bad bounce and smacked him in the face breaking his nose. I let him know that I had made sure to go ahead and field the ball to keep our goal intact and hold the batter to first base. He did not think that was very funny. I cringed even more, when two weeks later a hot shot was hit toward third base again and hit the same hump of ground, took the same bounce and even had the same results, breaking Joey's nose for a second time. This time I did not tell him that I was able to throw the guy out at first as the ball bounced off of his nose and right to me. I was later moved to catcher for a few games. Since I had not played the position before, opposing coaches tried to have their players steal bases against me. One tried to steal third. I threw the ball to Joey and as the guy was sliding with metal spikes toward the glove, one of the spikes wound up in Joey's hand causing a gash that required stitches. Joey did hang on for the out. He had a season of injuries but always laughed it off, came to every practice and had an amazing attitude.

As with many small towns, most guys try all the sports. Joey and I did play some basketball for the Aggies. We were both guards. One night in a tenth grade (JV) game on the road at Scottsboro, we sparked a second-half comeback that led to a victory. However, we were probably best known for our tennis. As seniors, I played number one for the Aggies and Joey number four in singles, but together we played number one doubles, compiling a 20-4 record in the classification for the largest schools in the state. Our friendship would continue to grow as our faith in God also grew. We were both members of the Fellowship of Christian Athletes and shared our testimonies at local churches. We generally stayed out of trouble but raised a few eyebrows when as seniors along with three of our good friends, performed in a high school talent show. Well, "performed" might be an overstatement. We lipsynched and phantom played instruments to a few songs of "The Beach Boys." We would call ourselves "The Beach Bums." We were apparently a hit as we performed with bizarre outfits featuring boxer shorts that had monkeys and hearts on them. The assistant principal, a tall gentleman named Tommy Lacks, walked into the dressing room as we were getting ready and doubled over, having to sit down on the bench when he saw our attire. Mr. Lacks was one of those administrators that although he was strict, most kids did enjoy him. He had a good sense of humor. He carried a set of keys that must have had a key to fit every door in the school. He had to attach it to his belt.

He even grinned at the running joke that if he removed the key ring, he would start leaning the other way as his body adjusted to the weight difference. My dad came to the talent show not knowing what we were going to do. People around him later told me he was red in the face, and crying, but it was from laughing so hard. We took an honorable mention, tying a concert cellist. She was not too happy with the results. I did not blame her. She actually made a career of playing in orchestras. I guess at that time humor still had a place in the talent realm.

This was all about the time that I had started dating the cute sophomore, Kathy Beam. Joey and I would go to our separate colleges. Joey went to Jacksonville State to study accounting and I went to Jefferson State and then the University of Nevada, Las Vegas to continue my tennis adventures. We would see each other in the summers. Kathy's younger sister Karen was working at the Martin Theater, a stand-alone movie house in town. One afternoon Joey asked me if I could introduce him to Karen. Kathy and I did just that. It seemed like a great idea at the time. Joey and I were great friends and dating sisters seemed like a natural. Joey and Karen clicked and fell for each other. In June of 1982, they were married with Karen beating her older sister to the altar by six months. Next, they beat us in having kids, presenting Mr. and Mrs. Beam with their first grandchild, Zac in May of 1986. Our son Gabe in February of 1987 became the second. We did have the third as Alex arrived in February of 1989, five months before Cassie arrived to Joey and Karen. Things were going along fine as Joey pursued accounting and I was selling real estate. He must have sensed that Mr. Beam was beginning to favor me as the favorite son-in-law because Joey decided to leave the accounting field to become a minister and the rest is history. So to paraphrase old Robert Burn's poem about mice, it seemed like a good idea at the time. In the case of the mice to build their nest where they did in the field and in my case introducing Joey and Karen, a move that would send my personal stock in Mr. Beam's eyes spiraling downward for years to come. If only at seventeen Joey would have set off to fulfill his dream of being a Solid Gold Dancer maybe things would be different.

I AM NOT LEFT-HANDED

One of my favorite movies is The Princess Bride. In a classic scene Inigo Montoya, the swordsman extraordinaire, is doing battle with the man in black. Inigo was attempting to make the fight fair by dueling left-handed, his less coordinated appendage. As the strategy of fighting left-handed is beginning to backfire he starts to smile. When asked why by his opponent, he replies that he knows something the man in black does not know. Inigo then shared, "I am not lefthanded." He quickly changes to his stronger side and begins winning the battle. Moments later it is the man in black's turn to surprise Inigo, when after also battling left-handed, he changes as well, saying that "I am not left-handed either." The man in black goes on to defeat Indigo. Later they become friends and work to save Princess Buttercup and yadda yadda. There is no point here other than to say that I am not lefthanded. However, is there possibly any doubt or any wonder that Mr. Beam is a southpaw? Maybe this explains some of the interesting twists of life that fill his days.

So this story begins a long time ago (the 1980's) in a place not far away. The home of Mr. and Mrs. Beam is the site. Visiting newlyweds from Roswell, Georgia, the daughter we will call Kathy and the second favorite son-in-law (me) have arrived for the weekend. Sunday morning church time was fast approaching and I was once again struggling to get dressed. One thing was stopping me cold. It was the same thing that stymied me time after time. The tying of the tie had me in a total panic. How could I be the son-in-law that Mr. Beam desired if I could not look proper for Sunday preaching?

After seven or eight attempts, I decided to swallow my pride and ask Mr. Beam for some help. I mean this guy wore a tie several times a week. It should not take but a moment. As I mentioned my dilemma, I tried not to make eye contact. I could not bear the thoughts of him glancing over at Mrs. Beam with that "my son-in-law can't even tie his own tie look." Then he asked me what kind of knot I would prefer. I was confused. I responded rather sheepishly that a regular knot would be just fine. I was thinking at this point that he had in mind to prepare the hangman's noose knot or something to that effect. He then proceeded to inform me of the various knots and that they all had different looks. I could have the Windsor, half Windsor, Trinity, Murrell, Balthus, Eldredge, Prince

Albert or he supposed the Simple knot. I mentioned that I thought that "bathtub" knot sounded interesting. He replied, "You mean Balthus." The more I thought about it the more I thought that this might be a mistake and then said, "let's just go with the simple." I heard either a sigh of relief or a sound of exasperation, sometimes I cannot tell those two apart.

Mr. Beam started by placing his tie around his neck with the skinny side on his right about one-third of the length of the wider part of the tie that was now hanging to his left. The only thing to this point that I was pretty sure about was that I had been told that the little side goes on the left. Mr. Beam had his on the right. Maybe this was my problem in all of those illfated attempts. I had the wrong starting point. Suddenly Mr. Beam begins winding the tie around and around while beginning a very bizarre exhortation. "Rabbit ran around the tree the fox was close behind. Round the tree they ran again, one more time. Then quick under a bush, the rabbit quickly fled then he took a giant leap over the big log ahead. The poor fox could only watch as the rabbit jumped in, a hole that led to the safety of his cool dark den." Mr. Beam was smiling proudly at the beautiful knot he had just tied. I was staring in the mirror with my mouth open shaking my head and asking, "what was that?" Mr. Beam could not believe I had never heard of the rabbit and the fox tie tying method.

Now over the years, I did learn that Mr. Beam did not have all the words to the poem quite right, but the moves were all correct and the results were without question. I assured him that unless the Steve Miller Band, Fleetwood Mac, Lynyrd Skynyrd, or even Parliament and Funkadelic had put those words to music then I had not had the pleasure. We both had a problem. I did not understand the lyrics and Mr. Beam could not tie the knot without them. So we started from scratch. I asked which side of the tie was the rabbit the big side or the small side. He said the big side. I mentioned that a fox was larger than a rabbit and that made no sense to me. Mr. Beam then explained that the fox really does not move and that only the rabbit moves. I followed with the fact that the story said the fox was close behind like he was chasing the rabbit. He explained that without the fox the rabbit would have no need to run and jump in a hole and we could not learn how to tie a tie and for me to accept the fact that the rabbit was bigger and did all the moving. With that settled we stumbled onto another obstacle. I had the fox on the left side and he had the fox on the right side. We were looking into the same dresser mirror and we did not even have the same starting point. It then dawned on us that Mr. Beam had a dominant left hand and I was righthanded. We then thought that we would stand facing one another, using each other as the mirror. "Mr. Beam if I am your mirror," I started saying and debated whether to finish, "then you are probably thinking you have never looked so good." He did not enjoy my humor as much as I did. "Just stick with the tie and not the jokes", he countered. Somehow over the next few moments, my rabbit had gone around enough trees and jumped over enough logs and into enough holes that I had a knot in my tie. A slight problem occurred when I tried to tighten and spruce up around the collar. I noticed the fox was now longer and sticking out below the rabbit. Having no more patience and even less time, Mr. Beam showed me the old trick of shoving the fox into the shirt and hiding it from the world. We then proceeded to have a great service at Antioch Missionary Baptist Church. Mr. Beam felt it was best for me to stick with the one-knot tying strategy and to this day, a simple knot it is for the second favorite son-in-law of the Trinity knotted Mr. Beam.

MR. BEAM, LUMBERJACK

In 1983 Kathy and I purchased a home in Albertville, with the help of my father, a local real estate broker. It had recently been built and due to a rainy fall and winter, the yard had not taken hold. There were several tree stumps and not much grass decorating the muddy terrain. I was twenty-two and a klutz when it came to yard work. I knew how to mow a yard, but I was certainly no expert. In the five-plus years of dating Kathy and spending time around the home of Mr. Beam, I had noticed how much he enjoyed yard work. His love for nice landscaping showed with his flowers and precision height mowing.

On one visit to our home, Mr. Beam mentioned a particular tree in wthe back yard that he felt could fall in a strong wind. He mentioned it would be best to cut it down. Mr. Beam has more confidence in my landscaping skills than I do, I thought to myself. I did not have a clue about how to accomplish the task. I mentioned I would gladly give it a try but would need some help. I figured with the way his yard looked, he would be the perfect partner. Also, I thought, why not have a little bonding time with the father-in-law? The tree was about twenty-five feet tall but not too thick. First, I thought, we needed a saw. I was not about to get a chainsaw because they were too expensive and I had heard horror stories of lost limbs, but not of the tree variety. I was not afraid of work, but I was afraid of power tools, so I chose a saw that you would see a real lumberjack use, a two-man saw. Mr. Beam was to be the second man.

At the sight of Mr. Beam and me taking the saw and trudging out to the tree, Kathy decided she would show wisdom beyond her 20 years of age and leave for a while. As she pulled out of the driveway with Mrs. Beam as her co-pilot, she witnessed the two of us tying a rope around the tree. I was up on a ladder wrapping the rope about eight feet from the base of the tree. I placed it above a couple of limbs to keep it from sliding down. You must understand, there was no Google search or even the Internet to look up how to projects. I was flying by the seat of my pants. I even checked to see which way the wind was blowing. Next, we had to determine which side and where to start sawing. I convinced Mr. Beam that the best way would be to cut the tree from side of house to side of house instead of toward the house or away from the house. I figured we had at least a 75% chance of not hitting the house that way. I also thought the best way to cut down a tree was to start sawing on the opposite side of the way you want it to fall and that when you got halfway or so, you started pushing it to fall in the direction away from the cut.

As I placed the teeth of the saw against the tree, Mr. Beam mentioned that we should go as low as we could to keep from leaving a large stump. That too seemed logical. This proved to be tough physically, especially for our backs, as we bent as low as possible while pushing and pulling the saw back and forth. The first fifteen to twenty passes did not show much progress as the outer bark proved to be a bit stubborn. I also just did not feel that I was getting a good enough push. I analyzed the situation and realized that the left-handed Mr. Beam was on the side where he was using his right hand as dominant and my left hand was getting more work. We laughed about it for a second and Mr. Beam mentioned that maybe we should cut from the other side of the tree and that way our hands would be correct. As we started that way, it dawned on me and I suggested, "why don't we just change sides of the saw? That should work." We changed sides and suddenly we were making progress. We got through the bark in no time and were beginning to see the light brown areas of the inner part of the tree. We were feeling pretty good about things when a strange thing happened. As the entire width of the saw entered the tree, the tree grabbed the saw. That is the only way I know to describe it. The tree decided to protect itself and trapped the saw in the midst of our thin incision. The tree was like a vice grip. We could not move the saw. It was stuck. Mr. Beam suggested that I go pull on the rope and see if we could get enough of a separation to remove the saw. To do that, I would need to pull the tree toward me. This should have been the first clue that I might not be Mr. Beam's favorite sonin-law. I mean here I am about to pull a tree on top of myself so that his daughter could find her a real husband, one that knew how to work with tools, somebody like his daughter Karen had found, someone like Joey. Not to be disrespectful, I decided to go ahead and give it a go. I was betting on the fact that when I pulled the tree down, my lightning-fast tennis reflexes would enable me to escape, shattering Mr. Beam's little plot. As I began to pull on the rope, I realized that my 145 pounds were not much of a threat to the tree. I literally turned my back to the tree and pulled the rope over my shoulder acting like a horse trying to pull a stuck carriage from a mud hole. By the way, Mr. Beam was no Hercules either. I was thinking that I had given enough space to remove the saw, but pull as he might the saw was not going anywhere. I then had an idea and before you know it, I had come from the house with the fix anything tool, WD-40. I sprayed the lubricant anywhere I could, into the tree incision, on the exposed part of the saw, anywhere. I then marched back and tried the horse maneuver again as Mr. Beam tried to loosen the trapped tool. I was hoping that this was not going to be a repeat of the famous "Sword in the Stone" story and that at any moment Joey was going to show up in a King Arthur type role, pulling the stuck saw from the tree and being the hero. Mr. Beam's voice brought me out of my daydream. "Got it," he said.

As I made my way back to the saw, Kathy and Mrs. Beam drove around the block to check on our progress. They did not say anything. They did not even wave. I think I noticed two heads shaking back in forth in the car, kind of like the old bobblehead dog on the dashboard of my granddaddy's pickup. Later she told me that they figured we would have certainly been done after ninety minutes. Next, Mr. Beam suggested that we make a second incision to keep the tree from collapsing on the saw. We started sawing a few inches above the old mark. I don't know if it was the WD-40 creating less friction or if we were getting the hang of the two-man saw, but we were quick to the same spot as before and beyond. Then it hit me. With the wedge the way it was cut out, the tree due to gravity was more likely to start to fall toward the open wedge cut and closer to the house and cars. We talked about the possibilities and decided to see if we could cut past the center and then push the tree in the direction we wanted it to fall. A few minutes later we had cut through about two-thirds of the tree. Fortunately, it had not yet destabilized on its own. We decided to push the tree. Mr. Beam even suggested that I get the rope and pull it again. This time I declined as I was now thinking about how much he must have disliked me, wanting me to pull the tree toward myself as he pushed. But when he said that he would pull and I push, I realized I had just been paranoid and that he was not thinking due to exhaustion. I suggested we both continue pushing. We actually heard a little crackle in the tree as we tried to guide the tree to our desired location. We decided to attack the tree from the opposite side and sawed that way for a little bit with the newly discovered wedge method, hoping it would weaken enough to make the tree lean away from the cars. We started, then stopped and laughed, "oh yeah, wrong hands again," we said as we changed to our more he-manly sides. We sawed some more from the other side but the tree was not moving. Now we were really getting tired and although neither verbalized it, we really did not care which way the tree fell as long as it fell. Kathy and Mrs. Beam passed by again, this time just blowing the horn as they glanced in the backyard to make sure we were still standing. They could see the tree sure was. She thought it looked as if a beaver had been chewing the tree. It was true, both sides were sawed away and the tree still stood tall with only a strong middle portion holding it up. Mr. Beam and I could not believe it was still standing. It reminded me of a quarter that had somehow balanced on its edge and the slightest movement would knock it over. We decided on the push method. Just pushing one direction did not seem to work. We then decided to start rocking the tree back and forth, hoping to get this project completed. We heard some crackling and felt a the tree give. We took this as a good sign and moved in for the kill. We pushed the tree again and it began to lean ever so slightly, and then a little further. Once more we pushed and finally, the tree fell toward the earth. As the top of the tree hit the ground the impact caused the trunk to bounce into the air above the newly formed stump creating quite the rush as Mr. Beam and I jumped out of the way.

We had done it. We had completed a fifteen-minute project in just less than two and a half hours. Now we looked at the tree lying across the yard, all twenty-five feet of it. What in the world were we going to do with this now? I looked at Mr. Beam and got no argument from him when I said that I would take care of that another time. Three days later the remainder of the tree was stacked in small neat pieces by the road. It took two knowledgeable men with chainsaws about ten minutes to finish the work. They charged me forty-five dollars. I asked how much it would have been to have them cut down the tree as well. "A tree that small, another fifteen would have covered it." The words of my dad rang through my head. "Son, you will always come out ahead to pay professionals for work that you know nothing about." I have since held strong to that advice. That was the first time Mr. Beam and I had worked together on a landscape project. In the thirty-seven years that have followed, we have not attempted another. I do not see that changing anytime soon.

PERSONAL CONFESSION #1

Before Kathy and I had kids we did the normal things that young marrieds do. We would go to the movies, to pizza restaurants with friends and to watch the local high school sporting events. Adding children to the mix of the family dynamics just seemed like the next logical step. I know that even way back then there were many books on raising children. I chose to ignore all the opportunities of page-turning enlightenment and just looked at Kathy and how she turned out. I figured if Mr. Beam could raise such a great person, surely I could handle it. I just needed to avoid creating another Joey and everything should be fine. The world only needs one of him. So I thought I would wing it.

Kathy and I attended some childbirth classes as the time drew near for her to deliver our firstborn. I never went with her to any of her appointments with our family practice physician that at the time still delivered babies. Everything seemed to be going okay and I felt that if the growth of the mom over nine months was any indication of a baby's health that we were going to have a very healthy baby. One particular Friday morning, Kathy was getting ready to go for her doctor's visit. I was much more interested in getting to the real estate office and seeing if I could sell a property to help provide for the new mouth on the way. She instinctively told me that she thought that I should accompany her on this particular visit. I reluctantly decided to go with her. She was close to her due date, but it was not quite time and thus I was not anticipating Dr. Belyeu's words. "I think you had better go home, get your things and head to the hospital." He went on to mention that Kathy's water had broken and he felt we would be parents soon. None of my sports training of remaining calm during big moments of contests came back to me. Over the next thirty minutes, Kathy remained cool and in control and probably should have driven. I was speeding through town, going airborne over railroad tracks with a very expectant mom attempting to get to the house, grab a suitcase and race to the hospital. The one thing I wanted to do is make it to the hospital on time and avoid delivering this child on my own. We got there, got checked in and were taken to a birthing suite. Kathy was hooked up to a couple of monitors and her vitals were being checked frequently. I was feeling a little better and my parents, Mr. and Mrs. Beam and a few friends started to gather in the waiting room. I would go back and forth telling people of the progress.

The date was February 6, 1987. From the hospital window, I could see the cold rain falling outside and the wind blowing one of those huge American flags flying over a nearby gas station. The television was announcing that it was President Ronald Reagan's birthday. When I read the USA Today, I discovered that Babe Ruth had also been born on February 6th. It might be a dad thing, but I felt all along that we were going to have a boy. We were not certain and had names picked out either way. A little girl would be named Samantha Jordan (Sammie Jo) Henderson and a boy would be Gabriel Gordon Henderson. Gordon was my father's name and my middle name so I thought we could keep it going. I began to think about the famous people sharing the birthdate with my child and thought to myself how old Ronald and Babe were going to be thrilled with what February 6th was going to offer up for the next generations to revere. Early afternoon Kathy, without the aid of any pain meds or epidurals birthed the eight pounds eleven ounce Gabriel. I ran down the hall with a patented tennis fist pump and informed the waiting room and anyone else in a one-block radius that, "It's a boy!" For the rest of the day, I did not care about work, play, or anything but the fact that I was a father to a little boy and Kathy was doing well. My whole world had stopped. A funny thing though, the rest of the world didn't stop. I mean I get it. It can't. I just thought that it should stop and take a look at my son. I have told both Gabe and Alex many times that you really cannot understand unconditional love until you see or hold your own child for the first time. It is such a reminder of how much God loves us. He gave us His very own son as a sacrifice for our shortcomings so that we can spend eternity with Him. It is truly Amazing Grace.

The next morning, Saturday, I went to the hospital for a while and began to realize that Gabe enjoyed sleeping. Kathy graciously allowed me or begged me to go play basketball with the guys. I took my bubble gum cigars and passed them out to the guys proudly. After a couple of nights, the staff at the hospital showed us the door and handed us this person to take home and take care of. Suddenly I was beginning to wonder if perusing a page or two of a parenting book would have been a good idea. As we began our life together, every noise or movement from the bassinet near our bed received our full attention. It was a few nights with limited sleep as we were determined to be there for Gabe's every need. Soon, as you adjust to the sound of the ceiling fan or the train blasting its horn through the town at all hours of the night, you become accustomed to the newcomer's sounds. The cry is the one thing that brings you out of your slumber to feed or change as needed.

In the fall we had some friends over on a Friday evening. We could hear the excitement from the high school football stadium about five blocks away. One of our friends thought it would be fun to walk over and check out the action. Everyone was in agreement and as we exited the back door it hit me and I looked at Kathy and said, "We forgot about Gabe." We had indeed, everyone had. The seven-month-old was upstairs asleep with his monitor on and the one-time future parents of the year had momentarily forgotten he even existed. Fortunately, the girls graciously decided to stay at the house and the guys went to the game vowing not to stay too long.

Gabe in the first year took most of his baths and spent most of his waking hours downstairs. One night I was preparing for bed as Kathy was bathing Gabe in our bathroom. I sleep in gym clothes. I am just not a pajama guy. I have always thought if anything happened, I would not have to waste time putting on a bathrobe or changing clothes. I would be ready to handle the situation. I rinsed my face, grabbed my toothbrush and picked up the toothpaste on the counter. Opening wide, I begin to scrub my pearly whites. This time something didn't seem right. Kathy must have gotten a different toothpaste brand. It was bright white and a little thicker than normal and did not have the minty taste I had grown to love. I looked down at the tube. It was white with writing on the back as I was staring down. Yes, the top was the same as my toothpaste, so I thought "oh well" and began to scrub some more. This time the taste, feel and texture let me know something was indeed wrong. I picked up the tube turned it over and realized I was brushing my teeth with Desitin ointment, not only that, it was maximum strength! Kathy had been applying it on the youngster to help with his diaper rash. The reason Desitin ointment was created was to stay on the surface of the skin and repel water. This cream was all over my teeth and in my mouth. You cannot rinse the stuff out. Water slips off your lips and tongue like a raindrop rolling off a freshly waxed car. I tried a towel and for the next few minutes did everything I could to remove the goo from my teeth. I did not get it all and was a bit concerned over how much Desitin ointment had slid down my throat. Kathy was not much help. She was laughing so hard she was crying and claimed she was holding Gabe and could not help with my particular predicament. I really think she was just enjoying the show. I could not drink normally for a couple of days. If I tried to drink from a cup or glass in a normal manner, water would hit my lips and slide around my face as the Desitin did its magic. I had to literally pour the liquid toward the back of my throat in order to get it into my system. I will say for the next week I impressed a lot of folks with my shockingly bright smile.

Now thirty-one years later crazy stuff still happens to families. I have a fellow Civitan and ALFA insurance agent friend named Jason Simpson. He and his wife Natalie have three children. Jason is in his early thirties and a former wide receiver for Kentucky Wesleyan University (I mention KWU because for years he has promised me a sweatshirt from his alma mater and I was hoping this would serve as a reminder and would shame him into making good on that statement). Jason also helps each year with our City of Albertville Christmas Parade. This year as we gathered as a parade committee early one morning at Jamoka's coffee shop, Jason would look away from the person talking and down at his phone which was silently ringing and then buzzing as text messages popped onto his screen.

He finally excused himself to take the call. After the meeting, he came over and mentioned that it was Natalie calling. It seems in the Simpson household that Natalie is the daily organizer for the family. Jason's daily regimen of vitamins, supplements or whatever are laid out on the counter each evening for him to take in the mornings. Apparently, on this particular morning, Natalie was missing her daily pills and was questioning Jason about which pills he took. Jason is a redhead with a fair complexion, but suddenly he was looking more pale than normal as he asked with sincerity, "Do you know of any side effects that a guy might have if he takes a birth control pill?" Without hesitation, I asked him if he had a sudden urge to shop, eat chocolate or get his nails done. He left the coffee shop a bit confused and bewildered maybe he was getting in touch with his feminine side. Maybe it was the talk about the Christmas parade, the overall mood of the holiday season or something a little more connected to the accidental ingestion, but that particular day turned out to be the most dollars spent on his credit card during the entire Christmas season. So watch out guys and make sure what is on the counter, women all over might attempt to see if the same results will happen with you.

PERSONAL CONFESSION #2

I am not a handyman. There I said it and it is in the open for all to know (as if my family did not already know it). I grew up in a small town, but not on a farm. My dad was in the real estate business and we had a home close to town and near his office. I grew up playing little league baseball, basketball and enjoyed riding bicycles to different neighborhood sandlots to hone my athletic skills. I eventually settled on tennis as my primary sport, but still enjoyed all the opportunities of throwing, catching, shooting or hitting a ball in various seasons.

As I aged, I began to understand that no matter how hard I tried, a flathead screwdriver was going to have a difficult time dislodging a Phillips style screw. Two things that I have found the ability to use and to use well, you might even say I have mastered, is the art of repairing anything and everything with duct tape and WD-40.

The most famous incident occurred in the wee hours of a morning in the early 1990s. My sister, Cindy and her family lived across the street from Kathy and me. I received a call from a frantic sister stating that water was shooting up in the middle of her yard and she did not know what to do or how to turn it off. Not one to back down from a challenge, I started out ready to save the day, I mean night. Sure as Cindy had mentioned water looking like a fountain was shooting about four feet into the evening air. A spicket head had broken leaving the mess. Now right now you are saying to yourself, spicket, I thought it was spigot. That is my point; I did not even know what I was attempting to repair. However, in the South many people pronounce it spicket and even old Webster himself points to a Middle English word spyket, but unfortunately spicket is not a word unless you use the urban dictionary. I am from a quite rural area. So the spigot was broken and water was flying and I attacked the issue hoping I could find a place that a wrench could work but spotted none. The next thing I could think of to use on the broken PVC pipe was one of the other two tools I had carried to the fight, duct tape. I could see no use for WD-40 in this instance, but I was prepared just the same. I assessed the size of the gusher much like I would an injured ankle of some of the tennis players I have coached. I would use pre-wrap and athletic tape to strengthen their joints.

The injured pipe in front of me would require the first strip of duct tape to be maybe six inches in length. I wrapped it around the half-inch pipe several times to give us a starting point. In no time, I had pinched the duct tape and made the perfect tear from the roll. The pipe wiggled slightly as I wound the tape around and around leaving just a little tape showing above the top. With the starting point in place, I next made a duct tape cigar by placing a significant strip in my hands, adhesive side out and begin to roll it back and forth until it was small enough to fit into the hole, but not too small that it would slide down inside the tube. I needed the adhesive to stick to the sides. As I began placing the tape cigar into the gushing pipe, water sprayed in all directions soaking me. I was not giving up though. Undeterred, I successfully filled the plastic cylinder and the adhesive was clinging to the side. Now the water was barely flowing. In a couple of minutes, I had followed up with several duct tape strips across the top and around the sides. Water was not escaping. The plumber hired to repair the spigot after assessing the situation and after about five minutes of laughter conceded that "well, it did stop the leak." Since that evening I have been the proud recipient of everything duct tape. Duct tape calendars featuring 365 ways to use duct tape (none of the days featured repairing a broken spigot), tee shirts with funny duct tape sayings, pink duct tape, camouflage duct tape and even rolls with college football team logos all came my way on birthdays and Christmas. I really don't mind, I still think it can fix anything. Just last year I used some traditional gray duct tape when the headlight of my silver 2005 Pontiac Aztek decided to pop out. I did such a good job matching the color and placing the strips that it took about 3 weeks before anyone noticed. I finally took it to an auto shop and got a clip to do it properly, but you get the idea. Duct tape and me, we stick together.

PERSONAL CONFESSION # 3

I really have a soft heart. I may hide it well, but it is soft. With few exceptions, I do not like to see anything suffer or mistreated. One exception is a fire ant mound. I just do not like fire ants. I do not understand their reason for existence. When I was a kid in Albertville, AL, fire ants had not migrated northward to our town. I could play barefoot in the yard and really only had to watch for a few kinds of grass with thorns and patches of clover that the bees like to visit, but overall, dirty feet was the major issue. My feet were tough and tanned. When Kathy and I moved back to Albertville in the 1980s, I began to notice these strange mounds of dirt rising from the soil and found out quickly that if you brushed into the mound that tiny ants with the passion of swarming hornets began to seek the perpetrator. Their sting would leave little blisters and itch for a week or so. Unfortunately, my nephew, Zac went to bed one evening with no worries only to awake the next morning to see ants covering his paralyzed legs. He had not been able to feel them as they attacked him. Somehow they had entered the house around the window near his bed and joined him. It was really scary and I am glad that he did not have an allergic reaction or was hurt even more than he was. So, I have rarely been barefoot since. My tennis keeps callouses on my feet, but overall they are soft and very white. So while this story starts with fire ants, it is really not the confession I wish to make.

The number one girl player on the 2017 Aggie tennis team that I coached, Meagan Moore would tell you that I do not like dogs. She would say that I do not play with, rub their belly or rescue them from distress. However, she has only seen me around the canines when they get around the tennis court. There they make me nervous for everyone. If you bring a puppy to a tennis match, the kids are going to run to the cute furry friend and forget about concentrating on playing the match. Case and point; even Meagan's mom, Karen and her sister Courtney know this to be true. It seems they acquired a new little four-legged pet and decided to surprise Meagan by bringing it to the courts to show her. However, Meagan was playing a match at the time of arrival so they kept the new family member out of sight knowing that it would affect her concentration. Another thing that tends to happen when dogs visit the tennis courts is that they have a need to relieve themselves. There is no telling how many times I have had to wipe dog mess off of my shoe before entering the courts to begin to play. Heck, I even had to put up a sign at the courts that if your dog messes on the tennis courts to clean it up. Yes, I have cleaned up the courts many times. Dogs also get excited when there are big crowds and inevitably begin to bark even as the owners sweetly beg; "now Fido, you be quiet." When the ball leaves the court as a player knocks one outside the fence, a mad dash begins for me as I try to beat the dogs to the fuzzy sphere. If I win everyone gives me a hard time and the dog continues to snap at the hand that is about to throw the ball back into the court, but to fail means we have to get a new tennis ball into play replacing a slobber soaked one with teeth marks. Away from the tennis courts, I have a problem when I am walking in my neighborhood, minding my own business on the street or sidewalk and a dog comes barreling full speed with teeth bared, barking and growling at me. Look, don't come charging at me when I have not done anything. We will have problems. I am not saying Meagan's dogs would do this, but the secret is they do. And what about the neighbor's dog that they let out at two in the morning to do its business and then they leave it out barking and whining the rest of the evening. In spite of all of that, I do like dogs. I like quiet, well-behaved dogs that do not speak unless spoken to and come up to you with a wagging tail. I will gladly spend time with this dog. I will throw balls unto my arm falls off or his tongue drags the ground. I will rub behind the ears or the belly and scratch the back of my newfound furry friend.

All of this leads to a memorable day at my Northridge home, the same home that Hannah and Gabe now occupy. Here begins a mini-confession inside of this full-blown confession. I am highly allergic to longhaired cats. Mr. Beam's favorite son in law and his wife that we will call Karen owned one and kept it inside. I really believe they kept it so I would not be able to stay long if I ever dropped by. In about five minutes, my nose would start stopping up and another five minutes would see my eyes start to swell. The other possibility is that Joey kept it around thinking that it would zap my energy or vision so that he could beat me in Ping-Pong. Ha, ha, I would laugh to myself, it would take at least two cats to make that happen. So, at our house we had cats, but they were outdoor and helped protect our carport from critters of the creek. Of course, we had to step around the entrails of some animals that had met its doom, as our feline friends would place the limited remains of all sorts of creatures on the welcome mat for our approval.

There is even a story as to how we acquired our first cat. I was in the process of selling a warehouse in Albertville for one of my real estate clients. Apparently, a momma cat had found a way in and delivered kittens in the back dark portion of the 40,000 square foot building. All of them ran and hid when they heard me come except for one little black and white female kitten. Gabe was about five and Alex around three years old when I brought the kitten home for the evening. They were elated and immediately entertained. Using the cardboard box that I had found to transport the feline to the house, the boys began to make it a bed. After a few moments, a name surfaced. They chose the name Catwoman. We later had a friend that had a cat deliver a litter of kittens and we obtained a solid white cat that the guys named Batgirl. We had a pair of superheroes patrolling the yard and keeping away snakes and mice. Well as nature would have things, both girl cats found a male friend and each had a litter of kittens themselves. We took one male from each litter and the light gray with dark gray stripes was named Lightning and the multi-colored mostly brownish-gold one was called, you guessed it Thunder.

One afternoon, I watched through the back window at what appeared to be a game of catch that Catwoman and Batgirl were having with a field mouse. Upon closer observation, I realized that it was not a mouse but a chipmunk. The rodent was being tossed around and up in the air. When it fell to earth and tried to scurry away the cats would pounce and pin the friend of the Disney characters Chip and Dale against the ground. Then they would slowly lift a paw to see if it was there and let it breathe a little. I suddenly had visions of my growing up years with Alvin, Simon and Theodore cartoons along with the melodious sound of the Chipmunk's Christmas album in my head. I had to rescue the chipmunk, but how? I wondered what Dave would do since he seemed to understand chipmunks as he lived with the aforementioned trio.

I decided to save the little fellow. I ran outside and got between the two cats, one of which appeared to be preparing to backhand the stunned varmint. I saw an opportunity and before Batgirl realized it, I had scooped the chipmunk into my tennis reaction enhanced speedy hands. In the time it took for the cats to leap and swing a clawed paw trying to retrieve their meal, the still breathing ball of fur was tucked in my rolled up shirt tail, snug and safe. I sprinted up the deck stairs and called for Kathy to get the boys terrarium so we could nurse Alvin back to health. In that short moment, we had bonded so well that I had named him. I even imagined getting a little red shirt with a yellow A for him to wear. The boys would love him. The cats in the meantime continued to use my blue jeans as a scratching post almost climbing up the denim to get to Alvin. They were clearly not amused at the new twist to their day.

I looked at Alvin, breathing fast and shaking. I began to use my finger to stroke the little striped back as I comforted him. As I finished a soothing pat, Kathy came toward the door with the plastic encasement that had been used previously for a hermit crab and then two anole lizards. The lizards are a story to their own. I must have taken my eyes off of Alvin to reach for the door because he began to squirm. As I reached down to reposition him, he lunged toward me with a mouth showing an opening the size of my fist. How did his jaws open that wide? Then with the force of Thor's hammer, he snapped his teeth shut spearing my forefinger with those nails he had for teeth. The bite went through my fingernail and almost out the other side of my finger. What is worse was that he was holding the bite. He refused to let go. Kathy watched in horror, well not horror maybe in some sort of sick amusement, as I began trying to disengage my finger from the chipmunk's mouth. I began moving quickly around the deck and started swinging my arm hoping to sling this predator off of my finger. My arm was moving faster back and forth than a third base coach waving a runner from first to home. Finally, by sheer centrifugal force, the attacking creature was sent hurdling through the air toward the brick outside wall of the home. I glanced at my finger with blood flowing through a gaping (small) hole. Then I looked up and saw Kathy laughing so hard that she was doubled over. I looked to the right just in time to see the flying ball of fur hit the wall and kind of slide down to the deck. Once on the deck, it tried to scurry away. I looked at Catwoman and Batgirl and said, "he is all yours girls, get him." As I walked toward the door to go doctor my wound, I taunted, "I may just see you on the welcome mat, Alvin."

I have disliked those Christmas songs ever since. Once again I called my sister Cindy the nurse practitioner. She laughed a little too hysterically for my liking and finally assured me that she had not been made aware of any rabid chipmunks and I should be just fine.

So you see my heart is kind for animals and I try, but I always seem to get burned or bitten. It is kind of like the story of introducing Joey and Karen, it seemed like a good idea at the time.

PERSONAL CONFESSION # 4

My friend since childhood, Gil Bruce, would consider me just short of a terrorist. Gil lived two houses from me and being a year older, a lot taller, faster, and stronger used me as his personal whipping boy in outdoor wiffle ball and driveway basketball games. If the score ever got too close in basketball an "accidental" hard foul into the non-padded steel basketball pole would turn the momentum back into Gil's favor. He did not need much help. Gil was the high school starting quarterback and punter, a fantastic baseball player, a pingpong champion and played a little basketball. He is a member of the Marshall County Sports Hall of Fame due to his great high school and college baseball career at Jacksonville State University. With all of his talents, why in the world would Gil consider me a threat in anything, you ask? This is more of a modern-day threat. You see, when Gil and I both came back to Albertville after college to make our home and raise our families, we would join some other guys for a weekly lunch get together. On many occasions,

Gil would order a hamburger. I love hamburgers, but it is how Gil orders his that put an unspoken wedge between friends. Gil orders his hamburger; it is painful for me to say, with mayonnaise only. AAAAYYYYEEEEE!!!!!!

I have what is known in the "urban dictionary" as mayonnaisephobia or simply a fear of mayonnaise. I don't really know if it is a fear, although Kathy would argue to the contrary, as I run from the kitchen any time a container of the white condiment is visible on the counter. I would say it is more of a strong dislike, aversion, disdain or well hostility toward all things mayonnaise. I think it started when I was a kid and I overdosed with the slimy substance as my mom put it on everything she fixed for me from saltine crackers to a grilled cheese with hot mayonnaise creeping over the side. Now it gives me a bad case of the heebie-jeebies to be around even a sealed up jar. These days I make my banana sandwiches with just banana and bread. The taste of mayonnaise is certainly a part of the problem. The taste is like a mixture of eggs, oil and lemon juice or vinegar mainly because it is. The jars with lemon juice are just way too sour and the ones with vinegar do not make sense. Look, I like eggs. I will eat eggs scrambled, fried, boiled, poached or most of the traditional ways to cook them. But I don't pull a Rocky Balboa and drink them raw. Then you have oil. Who in the world would turn up oil and take a swig? A little in a dish with seasoning to soak in some Italian bread or maybe mixed with some spices for a salad, but not combined with raw eggs. Has anybody out there tried the vinegar diet, where you get some apple cider vinegar and take a couple of tablespoons of that a day? I have, and I am not playing that game again. My throat and stomach burned for quite a while. Lemon juice is barely better. I have lemon with my tea and even with water when eating at restaurants. I have consumed glasses of orange, apple, passion fruit, mango, pineapple, grape, pomegranate, or juices with blends of all of them. I have also not turned up a glass of lemon juice. Lemonade with plenty of sugar does not count. Am I making my point? Why would anyone think that those ingredients mixed together would enhance the flavor of a sandwich or dip or salad dressing or even deviled eggs for goodness sakes? That does not even get into the potato salad mustard versus mayonnaise debate. Of course, mustard is better. Don't even get me started on slaw. There is nothing worse than enjoying cabbage and then see it surrounded by a puddle of mayonnaise on or in a dish. I am a vinegar slaw guy. If mayonnaise did not exist tomorrow, my world would be much less stressful.

If the taste is not the culprit, then maybe it is texture. When you open the lid to a jar of mayonnaise, have you ever noticed how it is still wiggling for a couple of seconds after the lid is removed? Peanut butter does not do this, nor does ketchup or mustard. Frankly, it is a little unnerving to watch. Another disgusting characteristic is the sound it makes when you scoop some onto your knife or spoon. It is kind of a half slurp followed by a slight smack like a kid does before learning some table manners. It reminds me of the movie Indiana Jones and the Temple of Doom. There is a scene where Indiana, Short Round, and Willie are at the table of a young Maharaja in a small village in India. It is a feast of bizarre foods topped off with a dessert of chilled monkey brains. The sound of the spooning of the monkey brains had to be taken from a jar of mayonnaise, they are eerily similar.

I have come out of the closet with my phobia and now most of the people I come in contact with soon know that I do not like the white goo. There are several restaurants that I visit on a regular basis. For the most part, the owners, servers and everyone around knows that whatever I have to eat comes with no mayonnaise. There is one restaurant in town that has a jar of squeeze mayonnaise in the middle of the table. As I take my seat I subtly but swiftly move it to the far end of the table away from my view while Kathy rolls her eyes. When I go into a restaurant for the first time and am not familiar with their preparation, I am quick to add at the end of my order the phrase no mayo. I will say things like hamburger, well done with mustard and fries, no mayo, Kung Pao chicken no mayo, spaghetti with meat sauce no mayo or pizza with everything except mayo. Sometimes the server will look puzzled, smile and say things like, we don't put mayonnaise on our spaghetti. I will nod and say, "Good, I just wanted to make sure." Other times, Kathy can see their confusion and while patting me on the hand, looks at the server and explains my little issue.

Once I went public with my dislike for all things mayonnaise including all those chicken dips, dressings, and aioli sauces, I became an easy target for some jokes. My entire Small Group at church showed up with little jars of mayo at an evening get together. At another church meal on a Sunday night featuring sandwiches and fixings', the church folk kept walking by my table placing those little mayonnaise packets beside my plate. This night the joke was

84

on them as apparently the packets had expired and gone bad. They even had to make an announcement not to use the mayonnaise. I was inwardly smiling as the vile, offensive packets were tossed into the garbage, never to harm anyone again. I also found God's timing and sense of humor refreshing as He enabled me the last laugh that evening. My lunch buddies and I spend a lot of noon hours at a local restaurant owned by Nelva Contreras whose husband Jose is the chef. Jose occasionally brings us creations from his kitchen to test. On some of his new recipes, he warns the table while shaking his head saying, "This is not for Greg, it has mayonnaise."

I am from the south but not a big NASCAR fan. I know that sounds odd, but this year in my state of Alabama our very own Talladega 500 was sponsored by Hellman's mayonnaise. Everywhere you looked on the television screen and scoreboard was a jar of mayonnaise. Obviously, I only watched about two laps of that race before channel surfing to find a football game at Heinz Field, seriously how about that for irony, a game played on a field named for a brand of ketchup and mustard took the place of the mayonnaise race. Not only NASCAR but have you ever seen those romantic comedies where the characters are eating a sandwich of some sort and one of them gets a little on their face, then the other one sheepishly says while pointing, "you have something here" and then stops and reaches over, wipes the excess away with there hand? Then they gaze at each other for a moment while the hand is still there before they have a little kiss. Sometimes that happens for real. My beautiful wife Kathy was standing in the kitchen taking a quick bite of a sandwich as she was preparing to head out the door for an event when I came around the corner to give her a little kiss on the cheek. As I reached her, she turned her head toward me, those gorgeous green eyes shimmering like emeralds. As my gaze shifted from her eyes I beheld a white glob on the outside of the corner of her mouth. There was not a hesitation, not even a thought of me reaching to wipe it away. I just stopped, turned around and quickly dashed out of the room saying, "You might need to do something about that white stuff on the side of your cheek before you go out Kat." There are no telling how many special romantic moments that have been spoiled by mayonnaise throughout history.

It is also amazing at how many more people there are like me in the world. My son Gabe is actually worse than I am about mayonnaise. If I am an eight out of ten on the dislike monitor, Gabe is a ten.

Kathy chides him sometimes and says he is being ridiculous while at the same time I am saying with pride, "That's my boy!" My pastor at First Baptist Albertville, Chris Johnson is about a six out of ten on the mayonnaise fear monitor. He now openly confesses that he does not really like mayonnaise either. His words were like a light from heaven confirming that I am not a sinner or outcast for feeling this way, that many people have their own fears in life, most a lot more serious than a little white spread. I have spoken to maybe a dozen folks over the last year that hate mayonnaise and have just not come out and let everyone know. We are now starting a movement. We are seeing people that thought they liked mayo begin to change and realize they had just been going along with the crowd instead of standing against all things mayonnaise. They also realize just how good a sandwich can be without the stuff. If you are one of us, one of the many that are ready for a life without mayo, let me know and we can band together. There is strength in numbers. In the meantime Gil Bruce, I am ready. Let's go! Two out of three games of one on one basketball, if you win mayonnaise stays in our fair town, but if I win Albertville becomes a mayonnaise-free community. Boy, I know that pole is going to hurt, but victory will be worth it!

MR. BEAM AND THE MAN IN BLUE

Grandkids, Mr. and Mrs. Beam have four. When you live in the same town, you have the opportunity to go to grandparent's day at school, talent shows and sporting events. Youth baseball in the late spring brings out all the family to see how the youngsters are looking in their uniforms, how they act in a dugout, who their friends are and oh yes, to see if they can hit a fastball or field a grounder. Often times, as in my case, the parents coach their youngsters. I really treasured the time that I could spend coaching not only my sons but also the opportunity to work with other young people as well. I always let Mr. Beam know that I appreciated the fact that he came to watch me coach (I was just sure that was the reason he came).

Mr. Beam while, raising his two daughters, did not venture into the coaching world. As a matter of fact, the girls did not play sports in their younger years. Kathy played a little basketball and has enjoyed the game of tennis over the years. Karen seems to enjoy aerobics classes and fitness training. Mr. Beam has left the sports world mostly alone. He may have had many opinions on some of my baseball or basketball strategies, but he never shared them with me. This was more of a social setting for the Beams. They enjoyed the sunshine, people and of course, Mr. Beam enjoyed the cotton candy with a suicide drink (that crazy soda fountain mix of all the carbonated beverages minus the diet stuff over ice). I never heard him yell to the kids or at the kids. He would just smile and talk to them in the on-deck circle. When Alex would come to the plate, he would say things like, "come on Alex Paul hit that ball." Now he did not use the name Paul to rhyme with ball as most people think and many people would. He always calls Alex by both names. Mr. Beam's name is Paul Jerry and I think he kind of liked having a namesake out there.

The Albertville field where the game was being played featured a few bleachers behind home plate and some near each dugout. Many people brought their own lawn chairs and placed them around the field with different angles and views. Mr. Beam chose the bleachers right behind the home plate umpire. This night as the game got started, the parents seemed to be excited about the action on the field. It was one of those nights where I wondered if the opposing coaches had promised to take the kids on a weekend campout if they won because the parents acted like they wanted to win real bad. That certainly got our contingent excited and before you knew it, our regular season baseball game for the kids had turned into an all-out tension-filled, parent cheering (yelling), win or no quiet weekend battle. Soon the fans attention turned to trying to get some help from the umpire behind the plate as call after call would have cheers or jeers depending on which team got the benefit of the nearsighted (I mean nice guy) man in blue.

At some point in the game, a youngster foul tipped a ball sending it over the backstop and into the crowd. It landed close enough to Mr. Beam that his cat-like reflexes allowed him to gather up the lace stitched sphere and look for a space to throw it back onto the field so the game could continue. The lefty steadied his not quite athletic body and let fly a throw that did not make it the required height and hit the fence and was met with a clank. The ball then careened into the crowd almost taking out a mom wearing a shirt saying that her son played for the opposing team and her toddler. The surprised mom shot one of those "what do you think you are doing glances" at Mr. Beam while the jeers and catcalls about his throwing prowess resonated from the crowd. The umpire stared menacingly at him and I looked at Kathy and just shook my head. Mr. Beam just smiled and apologized finding his seat and watching as the toddler who had grabbed the ball was now crying because the umpire made her give it back so the game could continue. Now the jeers and catcalls were toward the umpire for being a bully and taking the ball. He tried to explain that the league budget would not allow him to place a new ball in the middle of the game unless a kid hit a home run and was awarded the ball. Mr. Beam later blamed the errant throw on the cotton candy saying the ball stuck to his hand as he was letting go.

As the game continued and the pressure built on the umpire, a voice was heard loud and clear from behind home plate telling the man in blue in no uncertain terms that he did not agree with the call he had just made. The umpire turned to the crowded bleachers, pointed at Mr. Beam and said, "I've had about enough out of you. One more word out of you and you are out of here." In this particular case, Mr. Beam was not the culprit, but the umpire as in so many instances thought he was right and for some reason just knew he had the perpetrator. Mr. Beam leaned back a little and did what he does in situations of absurdity, he laughed. The always rule following Mrs. Beam began to urge him to be quiet hoping to get the attention focused back on the game. She did not realize this actually threw her husband further under the proverbial bus with the umpire. Her words convinced the umpire that Mr. Beam was the culprit. All of this made Mr. Beam's laughter more vigorous. The umpire used the "so you think this is funny" line and looked as if he was about to take action.

By this time I had walked down the first base line to see if there was some way to help the situation. First of all, I did know that the umpire had the wrong man. From my vantage point, I could see the heckler but my team was in a tough battle and I may have already ruffled his feathers over some differences of opinions in the first few innings. I could not see a positive situation arising out of arguing with him about the virtues of the ever-pleasant Mr. Beam. I walked up to the umpire and stood beside him facing away from the crowd and quickly made up the only thing I could think of at the time. "I know this man, as a matter of fact, he is my father-in-law", I started. After a brief exchange where I accepted his condolences for my plight, I continued. "He has not been the same since he was diagnosed with Witzelsucht disease. It is kind of rare and we are still trying to figure out what to do." "Witzel what? I have never heard of that. Anyway, I am sorry man. Just see if you can keep him quiet", the umpire replied. "How about if I move him to the stands beside our dugout", I asked. He agreed and I motioned for Kathy to move the Beams to the other seats for the remainder of the game. Fortunately, no more foul balls were hit in his direction, but there was a voice still being heard from behind the plate. The umpire must have then realized his mistake, but finished the game amidst the heckling. After the game, he quickly came up to apologize to Mr. Beam for the mistaken identity. He now knew that Mr. Beam was not the loudmouth. As he was leaving he finished with "and I hope everything goes well for you." "Greg shared your situation with me and I will be praying for you." Mr. Beam looked puzzled (which is not unusual) and thanked him.

"What did you tell him, Mr. Beam inquired?" I explained that I mentioned the first thing that popped in my mind and that I might have said that you had been diagnosed with Witzelsucht disease. "You didn't," Kathy said with a balled up fist and a smile on her face as she punched me in the arm. "What is that", asked Mrs. Beam.

Kathy answered, "don't worry dad does not have it." I was listening to NPR (National Public Radio) on my way home the other day and they were talking about this strange phenomenon. When I came into the house I told Greg that I knew what was wrong with him, he had Witzelsucht disease and that the boys seemed to be in danger of catching it from him. I then shared my reason for the diagnosis. Witzelsucht is the neurological disorder whereby people make poor jokes, wisecracks or puns at socially inappropriate times. Now I am certain he has it." She then punched my arm again. "Hey!" I explained. "It was the first thing I could think of and I did not want your dad to get thrown out. I was also betting on the fact that the umpire most likely did not listen to NPR. I figured umpires prefer the blues. Get it Kathy, the blues, they wear blue." Apparently, she did. The third blow to the shoulder removed all doubt.

ANYTHING GOES WITH THE PROPER PROSE

I must hand it to William Shakespeare. That guy could flat out write and although I have not studied his works as I should, I do enjoy many of the phrases he penned. One of my favorites is from a Midsummer's Night Dream. I really do not know the context but it goes, "though she be but little she is fierce." Trying my whole life to be an athlete at 5'8" it stands to reason that those words would encourage me. I also loved the movie Seabiscuit. Jockey Red Pollard changed to the masculine the same line when referring to the small but swift racehorse that he rode. Another Shakespearian quote that catches my attention is "kill with kindness." It is from The Taming of the Shrew.

It appears that most Southerners were paying attention in this particular portion of their English Literature class. Opening the door for others, saying, "Yes sir" and "no ma'am," helping the elderly across the street or with their groceries among other things are still taught to our children. They may not act on their knowledge without encouragement, but once reminded they spring into action. I coached the local high school tennis team. Before and during the season, parents would bring water or sports drinks to the courts for the players and coaches consumption. Some of the cases can be quite heavy. One day a mom was unloading an SUV full of water for the upcoming matches. She started to bring the first case down the sidewalk. All I had to do was look at the players on the boy's team and say, "hey guys." They quickly assessed the situation and sprang into action. From that moment on, at least for that season, I never had to remind them. When someone came to the courts with something heavy, they took care of it. Two words, a simple reminder, and what they had learned and knew to do came back to them. Of course, the moms loved it. It is really not all that chivalrous of an act. I mean think about it, someone went to the trouble to buy something for you so that you can perform better and then brought it to the courts for you. Are you really going to ask them to unload it also? I think not, at least not while I am coaching. There are so many other examples. Sometimes when you ask if you can help in a situation the other party refuses the help or looks at you like you have a vicious ulterior motive. As Paul and Barnabas did in Acts 13:51 of the Bible when the people refused their help, they

96

just shook the dust off their feet as a sign of frustration that their goodwill was refused. That is what we Southerners have learned to do, just help the next person if possible.

The "kill with kindness" also transferred to Southern conversation and has become well known for allowing you to say anything about anybody as long as you remember to add a few special phrases at either the beginning or the end of the statement. I really think it started with aristocratic women that were smart enough to phrase their conversations in such a way that even though they were gossiping, they could get away with it as if they were not gossiping. Any conversation could go from gossip to non gossip by adding words like God bless him, God love her, Bless them Lord or good Lord willing. By adding those words it shows that you are pulling for the subject, praying for the subject or hoping the best for the subject being talked about. You can also add a bit of humor to a situation and get away with it as well, but you must be careful with that one. A southern conversation might go, "Did you hear about Johnny and Sally? God bless them, I heard they were expecting baby number seven. I did not think they would have anymore, seriously Johnny, God love him, will be 68 when this one graduates high school." The literal translation of what is being said goes something like this. "I just heard that Sally is pregnant. Can you believe that? They already have six kids and aren't doing a bang up job of parenting them. What in the world were they thinking? Johnny is just too old to be a baby daddy again. I really thought he got fixed after number six. I suppose that did not work." Of course the latter would be gossiping.

You can even use the Southern terminology with family members. A conversation might go something like this. "My oldest son, God love him, went to Las Vegas and came back with pierced ears and earrings. I was not terribly surprised; he had wanted to do something like that for a couple of years. Bless his heart." That really happened with Gabe. What I was saying was, "if he doesn't hurry up and grow out of these teenage years, I am going to lock him away in the attic."

My good friend and former worship pastor Chuck Johnston used some clever phrases to help diffuse his frustration and keep from saying something bad about someone else. He once introduced an old song with a new flavor to our church choir, a bridge he called it. He described the choir, "God bless them. They looked at me like cows staring at a new gate." Translation; aye yi yi, these folks don't have a clue.

MRS. BEAM GETS IN THE ACT

If you can't say anything good about anybody than just don't say anything is one of Mrs. Beam's favorite mottos to live by. She passed that down to daughters Kathy and Karen. Some of that has even rubbed off on me over the years. However, it is still tough to say good things about Joey. All he does is good things so I just choose not to say anything. Over the last few years, Mrs. Beam has shown signs of breaking under the pressure of always talking nice about people. She and Mr. Beam live on a quiet street in a typical small town neighborhood. On one summer day as Kathy and I were visiting the bird sanctuary with grass an inch and a half high, Kathy mentioned that the neighbors needed to mow their grass. It did look awful and looked abandoned except it was not. Mr. Beam had seen the perpetrators in their yard, smiled, waved and offered to let them borrow his lawnmower. That was his kind way of saying cut your grass, please. Mrs. Beam was more understanding, "They must have allergies and that is why it looks like that." She was way too kind.

My response was "yeah, allergic to sweat." About three weeks later they finally mowed. I did not see in the obituary section of The Sand Mountain Reporter or read on Facebook of anyone in town dying from the sinister grass-clipping allergy, so I thought my explanation had more credibility. On another occasion, Mrs. Beam spouted a classic don't say anything bad about people statement. Mrs. Beam spotted, and I am sure Mr. Beam did too, a lady with too much body for the clothes she was wearing. Mr. Beam was speechless but Mrs. Beam calmly surmised, "She must be hot natured." Our family has certainly used that quote many times over the years when we see scantily clad individuals about town.

It does not stop there. Mrs. Beam's goodwill has now spread to incoming telephone calls. If I receive a call from a number that I do not recognize or from a solicitation service, I do not answer, wish I had not answered or made the caller wish that I had not answered. Mrs. Beam, on the other hand, has come up with another plan. Since she typically reads the Bible every day, she has now started reading it to the solicitors. "I'll keep reading as long as they stay on the line. Sometimes they stay on for a couple of minutes, but most of the time they just hang up." The brilliant Mrs. Beam has come up with a perfect strategy. I am trying to get her to start a business. I think the Mrs. Beam dial-a-prayer or dial-a-verse of the day service would be fantastic. She is obviously good at it. The same number will call back two or three times a day. They might be hoping that Mr. Beam will answer, but I bet they have their coworkers calling to hear more from the Book of Deuteronomy narrated with a Southern accent.

MY THANKSGIVING TREAT

None of us old enough to remember the happenings of September 11th, 2001 can possibly ever forget that day. That moment in history changed so many things that we do. The ways that we travel, think, plan and live were no longer simplistic. I certainly do not want to make light of any part of 9/11 in telling the following story nor do I want to come across as an unsympathetic person. I was stunned like the rest of the world watching the twin towers fall to the ground and throwing us into a war on terror. Commercial aircraft were grounded. People were staying near their homes. I remember the next few evenings in Albertville were brilliant, crisp, autumn evenings, with clear star-filled skies. I stood in the driveway looking up talking to God, as I tried to wrap my mind around what was happening in the world. On most evenings I could look up and see several airplanes in a short amount of time. It seemed the airspace above our home was part of the approach used for aircraft traveling to and from HartsfieldJackson International in Atlanta.

You don't realize just how many planes are constantly in flight above and around you until they are no longer there. It was strange. I, like many others, wondered just what our future would be like in the United States. I remember President Bush with his charge to the American people to go about your lives and not be intimidated.

Kathy and I, along with our good friends John and Carol Slivka, had a very interesting decision to make. Carol, a hospital finance administrator was scheduled to attend a conference in Las Vegas on Monday the 17th. The rest of us were tagging along to vacation and see my old college town while Carol hit the classes. We decided to make the trip. We drove to Nashville, Tennessee to take the Southwest Airlines direct flight. It was spooky walking through the airport. It seemed as if we were in a dream and making the slow-motion journey to the gate through the mostly empty airport. An occasional slow turning head from another person waiting at a gate would make eye contact. The crazy thoughts ranged between what are we doing on this plane, too, I may be staring into the empty eyes of the next terrorist! Of course, security was strong but since there were no passengers it did not take anywhere near the two-hour pre-flight check-in that we were encouraged to allow. It was also a very speedy boarding process as the four of us and maybe twelve other passengers took our seats for the nonstop three and a half hour flight. The whole country was under a cloud of mourning and uncertainty and Las Vegas was no exception. In all the time that I lived there or have visited I have never seen it that empty and quiet. The hotels, the streets, even the cabs seemed to be on hold. We did try to enjoy ourselves and we did experience some great food and fun moments, but with our country hurting, it almost seemed like we were doing something wrong. I chose to think we were helping let others know that it was okay to travel and that we needed to listen to our President and keep living. The United States needed to stay strong.

A couple of months after the Las Vegas trip we were entering the holiday season. I decided to try and do something a little different for Thanksgiving. Now there is nothing wrong with spending Thanksgiving with Mr. Beam and Joey but this particular year I asked Kathy to let me arrange a family Thanksgiving. Gabe was fourteen and Alex twelve. I figured we would not have many more opportunities to do something with just the four of us. I was correct as Gabe's basketball skills placed him on a path to play high school basketball. The varsity squad had Thanksgiving tournaments that eliminated holiday weekend getaways for the remainder of his high school years. Kathy apprehensively agreed to let me handle the planning of the Thanksgiving excursion and was thrilled when I told her and the boys to pack for a couple of nights stay at the Opryland Hotel in Nashville, Tennessee. Man, who didn't like that place? It was and still is a very nice resort with amazing gardens; atriums, waterfalls and to top it off the Christmas lights would be displayed during our stay.

We arrived on Wednesday evening. With Thanksgiving less than twenty-four hours away the staff and guests alike were cheerful and in a festive mood. We had hardly registered at the front desk when we turned to see many people milling around the lobby. Suddenly a camera, a lighting pole and a microphone were placed in front of me as a newsperson mistaking me, I was sure, for Tom Cruise began an interview. Actually, he did not mistaken me for Tom Cruise but he was doing a feature story on holiday travel after the events of 9/11 and was quick to recognize by the suitcases and the family with me that we were travelers. The next few moments have lived in Henderson family folklore ever since. Gabe, Alex and I are quick to revisit and remember in our own versions what happened.

I looked down at the microphone and then up at the camera realizing that the time had finally arrived for me to showcase my on-camera talents. A person with a clipboard asked my name, which I felt sure would be onscreen under my picture on the upcoming ten o'clock news broadcast. The reporter then started the questioning with something like "I see that you are traveling with your family and we are wondering about the mood of travelers after the events of 9/11. Did you drive on this vacation or fly to Nashville and are you worried about possible terrorist activities this holiday season?" As I straightened my 5'8" frame to maximize my on-screen presence, I started the answer that we did drive from Albertville when I felt a nudge from behind and heard a voice as Mr. Beam's daughter (the one that we will call Kathy) popped into the shot and said, " we flew to Las Vegas the Monday after 9/11." The reporter heard Kathy's interjection and decided to go with it. Kathy recoiled a bit as I moved to my right and the camera once again followed me. The reporter then said to me: "wow, less than a week after the attack you flew, what made you decide to do that and how did it feel?" "It was a tough decision", I began my All-American and patriotic response, "but we felt it was important to follow President Bush's instructions to carry on with our plans and to not let the enemy strike fear into our nation." I was on a roll. I was about to describe the trip and you could sense the interest from the reporter when suddenly a voice then a body entered the camera shot. "The Nashville airport and the airplane we flew on were empty. It was a weird feeling." I heard Kathy before I saw that she had once again joined me in the conversation. She was smiling brightly and the green eyes were shimmering jewels. I gave her the ole husband-to-wife look. I wanted to say, "what are you doing, they are talking to me?" Truthfully though I knew she was the better looking one and if they started talking with her, my chance at being discovered would be lost. It didn't matter what I was thinking though, she was in Nashville with a camera and an opportunity to be discovered. It reminded me of the I Love Lucy show of yesteryear when Lucy would do all sorts of things to get an opportunity at stardom, usually at Ricky's expense. The rest of the interview is a bit of a blur as the reporter had a couple of follow-up questions and then some young female singer (that we will call Sara Evans) who had some sort of impressive album (that we will call Born to Fly) entered the lobby. The reporter and crew then left me faster than my lovely bride could tell them that her name was Kathy with a K. We stood there for a moment and then looked at Gabe and Alex reenacting the interview. Gabe was a stoic and stiff interviewee, I suppose making fun of his dad and Alex kept popping his head next to his brother's speaking in the soft, higher toned voice, presumably his mom's. Our next couple of steps led us to the elevator and our room for the evening. The gardens did not disappoint. We opened the balcony and listened to the waterfalls and echoing voices of guests walking along the garden paths. We tried to get to bed at a decent time. The family knew that as usual with my travel plans we would have a full day and start early, but they were not exactly sure what was in store for Thanksgiving.

Up at six, I was eager and energetic as the rest of the group groaned, placed the covers over their heads and said things like "seriously dad, it is Thanksgiving Day." I assured them I knew what day it was and that I had a plan. "Wear your jeans and a jacket," I urged as I rechecked my watch and calculated the time to the destination.

We would be traveling just less than 100 miles this morning and I wanted to arrive by 9:15 although 9:30 would be okay. I had topped off the gas tank the evening before. I had learned from a previous

Thanksgiving excursion to Chattanooga with the aforementioned Slivkas and their children, that food and fuel could sometimes be a challenge to find on the special American day.

We buckled our seatbelts and started the journey north on I-65 at 7:22 a.m. Kathy looked at me and the boys looked at each other when we crossed the state line leading into Kentucky. We passed through Bowling Green about 8:35. Gabe and Alex seemed a little disappointed as I chose not to take the exit to the Corvette Museum. Another half hour and we were turning onto Kentucky Highway 70 at the Park City exit toward Mammoth Cave National Park. The secret was somewhat out but the quizzical "whys" were still in play. "It will be great," I started. "And yes it is open on Thanksgiving, I checked. I even have reservations." Everyone was surprised that you had to have reservations to walk through a cave. I tried to explain that this was not any cave. "Mammoth Cave has more than 400 miles of passageways and is by far the longest that we know about in the world. I thought since we enjoyed Cathedral Caverns (a very neat cave that has been opened and closed throughout the years near Grant, AL) that we would love this one," I encouraged.

Now if I have made Kathy out to be anything but a warrior to this point then I have accidentally been misleading. She enjoys the term "boy mother" and she wears it well. She has hiked, caught lizards, obtained jars for scorpions, looked under rocks for salamanders, thrown Frisbee, played basketball, baseball, tennis, football and rolled in poison ivy only to wake up in an itchy, whelp infested body, all in the line of duty as a boy mother. As we were planning for a family, I had what I thought was the perfect arrangement. We would first have a boy, then two years later we would have another boy and then three years later have a girl. Kathy just kind of smiled with that "yeah right, sure" look about her as I shared the idea. It came to be that in February of 1987 that Gabe was born. We followed that in February of 1989 with the birth of Alex. This is great I thought, we are right on schedule. In February of 1992, we will have a little girl. As Kathy sat there sweetly holding young Alex and I leaned over to tell her that I was so happy that our plan was working to perfection she reached her right hand up toward my neck. I was sure it was for a tender kiss. Her right hand suddenly grabbed both sides of my button down collar and pulled me, blue eyes to green eyes. I was taken aback and frankly a little scared. The voice of a woman that is just a couple months removed from giving birth for a second time and thinking of another period of gestation and labor is downright frightening. "You can't guarantee that the next one will be a girl!" I started to reply but with the now constricted throat and lack of air circulating I sounded like Eddie Murphy in Trading Places as Dan Aykroyd was about to get revenge and instead of Murphy's "it was the Dukes," mine was "but I have a plan." The next day I scheduled my doctor's appointment so that the world would not have the worry of any more little Hendersons and Kathy could focus on being a boy mother.

We actually pulled into the parking lot at 9:13. Not that I was taking credit or anything about the punctuality. I mean I normally try to do my part, but I am always thankful to the good Lord when we are accident-free and do not have abnormal delays due to construction, speeding tickets or abnormal amounts of bathroom breaks. "Well," Kathy said with a surprised tone. "We are not the only ones here. I really did not expect to see anyone else. It is after all Thanksgiving Day and it is a cave." She quickly warmed up to the idea as she saw the tripod coming out of a small white van. The flip down passenger mirror reflected the exquisite Kathy as she quickly applied finishing touches to the masterpiece. She just knew that the news crew from last night had followed us up for a more personal interview of the fearless traveling family. Her disappointment was not contained when the tripod was set up for cool still photos of the entrance to one of the caves.

Our tour started on time. It was a four-hour tour that covered almost four miles of the cave. There were many stairs at the start as we descended from light into darkness. Immediately the boys were captivated by the sheer size of the cave. We had a great adventure as we made our way along with the others in the group. We passed the spectacular "Frozen Niagara Falls" stalactite and stalagmite formation. The passageways were quite spacious and typically getting around was easy. There were the occasional steps that could be trouble for some, but for our family, it was a blast. The guys could not believe that there were restroom facilities 200 feet below ground. Of course, we checked them out. The highlight came about noon when our tour entered a large chamber with picnic tables. With a dumb waiter system available the park rangers had set up a special Thanksgiving meal of turkey sandwiches and tomato soup for the tourists. We gave thanks and begin to eat. I think that I heard someone sitting beside me saying, "I could be at a large dining room table at my parent's house eating turkey, dressing and all the trimmings, but no, I am in a cave, on Thanksgiving." Have I mentioned about the boy mother thing? I looked at Gabe and Alex and said, "Don't worry she is having a blast". As we continued the journey I limped for a few hundred yards and rubbed my leg from being kicked. Upon completion of the tour, we headed to the car. We thanked the park ranger that led our tour and mentioned that we expected barbeque and baked beans when we were back for the Fourth of July. We got on the road and stayed in Nashville for another night before heading back to Albertville on Black Friday. We have enjoyed many Thanksgivings, but this one was the most unique to date.

DEFINITELY NOT
(A PARTRIDGE IN A PEAR TREE)

The wreath was artificial, not that I could tell the difference. It had a lot of greenery surrounding a brownish, circular, twiglike form. The one on the front door looked just like it. They were each adorned with the red ribbons and featured gold and silver highlights, letting everyone that looked toward our home know that it was the Christmas season and we planned on enjoying this time of year. But the wreath under the carport has most to do with this story. Kathy hung the wreaths in place on the doors in early December. It is a time of year that in North Alabama night falls about 4:45 p.m. I pulled into the carport, got out of my 2005 Pontiac Aztek and headed toward the entrance. The only light was coming through the wreath-covered window of the exterior door leading into the playroom; a faint glow to guide me up the three steps into the warmth. I grabbed the laptop case that still houses the same Mac Book Pro that is currently creating this best seller and started toward the door. A sudden swift movement about eye level captured my attention for a moment. A bat, I thought. Sometimes they dart down from the trees, diving toward a person until their sonar tells them to veer away.

I entered the home with my borrowed greeting "Honey, I'm home!" I borrowed the words from the movie Pleasantville. The George Parker character played by William H. Macy would enter the home every evening and his wonderful bride, Betty Parker played by Joan Allen would greet him at the door with a refreshing beverage and maybe a kiss on the cheek. After taking a sip George would ask, "Is that meatloaf I smell?" The movie would then continue. I do not live in the movie world, but Kathy would certainly make for an amazing leading lady. So, no beverage but a pleasant answer of "Welcome home!" greeted me as the door closed. That is certainly not a bad thing. I have no complaints when comparing the Henderson world to Pleasantville.

I made my way through the kitchen and into the family room. "Wow! The Christmas tree looks great," I said to Kathy. She was placing some finishing touches on the branches she had been decorating. I quickly noticed the place of honor of the various Georgia Bulldog ornaments. The ole Sammy Sosa ornament was sharing a branch with a little mouse on skis. Gabe and I loved watching Sammy Sosa chase history with the Cubs. We would turn on WGN and while he was still with us, we listened to Harry Cary tell us what he thought was going on in the contest. He loved the Cubs and for that time I loved major league baseball. I played in a couple of fantasy leagues and always finished near the bottom as I overpaid for my favorites and had to take several non-productive players to finish out the team. Then the whole steroid thing hit and I felt totally betrayed. I still think the owners were very much at fault. I think they knew what was going on in the locker room, but as long as it was filling stadiums and bringing in revenue, they did not care. When the league finally decided to take a stand the game had been forever tainted. After those WGN telecasts where Sammy would hit a monster shot, the reporters would interview him in English and he answered with clarity of thought and voice, then he goes before Congress during the steroid hearings, has an interpreter and suddenly cannot understand the language. I still like him as a baseball hero, but come on. I have watched very little baseball since. I don't guess I will. If the Braves get hot, I might turn them on for an inning or two. There are a lot of other ornaments, a bunch the kids had made in their earlier years of school and many from as far back as 1982. That is the year we got married and the ladies hosted an ornament shower for our December wedding. Our Christmas tree was an artificial tree due to my allergies but it looked very real. Kathy had mixed and matched the colors well on the branches. She tries to add a few things to spice it up like ribbons, angels, stars or new ornaments. I marveled at her use of real items. Pinecones adorned the green branches along with a fun looking bunch of woodsy animals.

The famous t-shirted vermin, Simon, Theodore, and Alvin, represented chipmunks. There were glass squirrels and an amazing looking bird on one of the outer branches. I pointed and said, "I like the bird, it's pretty cool. Is that new?" Kathy assured me that she had not purchased any new ornaments this year and that men just do not remember things like ornaments and who gave whom what gift in which year. I had to agree with her, but I could tell her that Sammy Sosa had 609 career home runs and his first was off Roger Clemens in 1989. I also remembered a whole lot of the scores from my Little League baseball games. A table lamp presented a soft glow for the room. I plugged in the lights for the tree, which resulted in a nod of approval. We sat and relaxed with a little Christmas music in the background. I watched as the holiday skaters in the

Hallmark ornament glided over the pond of their world. Other ornaments twinkled while some did nothing more than bring back memories of Christmases past. My mind was drifting and enjoying the moment. The world seemed to slow down for a change. I asked Kathy if she had a crick in her neck. She had twisted it a little toward the side of her body nearest the tree a couple of times and turned her head slowly. "No," she answered, "I keep thinking I am hearing something." We looked around for a moment and as is always the case, there were no strange or new noises. That is the moment the bird ornament at the edge of the branch moved, no it flew from its branch. IT FLEW FROM THE BRANCH! Snapping out of a temporarily frozen stance I realized that the bird was alive and now flying about the once serene living room. Kathy went to full panic mode, screamed and started making all kinds of suggestions to me about how to get the bird. I had my own plans. I first wanted to limit the bird's options. I closed all the doors that I could, which left the living room, kitchen, dining room, foyer and a long hallway for the bird to travel. Next, I analyzed the surroundings; let's see nine-foot ceilings in several areas but twelve foot vaulted ceilings in others. At my height all of this was important.

Kathy was not at all impressed with my strategic initiative. She wanted action. "Hurry and get it out before it leaves bird droppings everywhere." Only she did not say droppings, but before you think anything bad she did not say the bad word either. She said, "poop." I was trying to spare you from that but she was scared of bird poop. I did not understand. I mean, I know it is a little humiliating to be standing outside and a bird flies over while you are talking to someone and the bird confuses you for a statue and lets you have it. I also don't like to pull out after my annual car wash visit and see that a few birds have perched themselves on a power line above my car and seem to be targeting my door handle or the beautiful emblem of a Pontiac Aztek. Kathy, however, is not the only one that fears the flying scuz droppers. My fellow realtor, Emily Jennings and I were pulling weeds from the sidewalk of our Main Street office one morning when she suddenly shifted to another location, sighting a bird on the roof overhead. "I don't want to be pooped on," I believe is the way she said it.

Let us get back to the moment at hand. I have been running around the house trying to assure Kathy that if the bird poops a little in the house, it will be okay. We can clean it up, meaning I can clean it up.

I just wanted to determine how to remove the bird without hurting it or having another chipmunk incident. I opened the front door and then the back door that led to the deck. Surely the bird would feel the nice breeze and desire to be back in the great outdoors. Apparently, this bird had taken a liking to the Christmas tree and the comfort of the central heat and air. It headed to the kitchen and perched itself on top of the cabinets.

Next, I climbed onto the counter and stood. Of course, once I got into position, the bird flew toward the foyer. Kathy was encouraging me to be careful. I answered her plea, "If anything happens, make sure everyone knows that I was injured, maimed or killed battling a prehistoric Pterodactyl. They can never know the truth." I eased off the counter and once again set off on the quest. Birds to me do not seem near as dumb as the birdbrain insult often hurled at people would lead you to believe. They do some creative things. I mean the killdeer are pretty good actors. They usually lay eggs on the ground in camouflaged areas with rocks and dirt. They will see something coming close to their nest and then run a few yards away and lead you to believe they have a broken wing. This keeps dangerous predators away from the nest and chasing the parent. I was not dealing with a killdeer, but still, this bird had apparently assessed the enemy and developed a strategy involving altitude. The bird was staying perched high and out of my reach.

I had an idea. I walked by the sports closet that my golf clubs were in. I had momentarily thought about using a club to help with the bird, but I quickly realized that the golf clubs and I had not had much luck in getting birdies in the past. I went instead to the Aztek, lifted the hatch, opened my tennis bag and got out the HEAD speed pro racquet. It is the kind of racquet Novak Djokovic plays with. As I brought it to the foyer Kathy protested, "You cannot just smack it." That was not necessarily my plan, although when the bird flew right past me back toward the kitchen, the thought of taking a backhand practice swing did cross my mind. On top of the curtains above the kitchen table was the new spot the bird chose. I eased closer and opened a window hoping this time it would fly away. It did not. I raised my racquet gently toward the winged intruder and placed it right at the feet. Curiously the bird responded by placing one claw on the strings of the racquet and then the other. It was now standing comfortably on the racquet near the apex of the HEAD symbol. I turned and moved slowly toward the door and once I stepped onto the porch, the door slammed behind me. Kathy was taking no chances. I moved the racquet quickly up and down three or four times until the bird turned loose and flew toward an oak tree branch. Once back inside the home, I closed all the doors and windows and scoured the home for bird poop. Finding none, I declared that all was well.

The next morning as I headed out the carport door a fast flutter of wings and a swooshing sound greeted me. It was then I realized that the bird from last evening was making a home in the wreath at the carport door. Kathy and I discussed what to do about it and chose to monitor the situation. Guys usually do not talk about adventures like we had the previous evening, but apparently, women think it is all right to do so. They even poke fun at the man attempting to catch the perpetrator.

Kathy and I left for our day's work. She beat me home by a few minutes and was busy about the house when I arrived. After the before mentioned greetings, I walked toward the family room and toward the Christmas tree to rest a bit. My eye caught a glimpse of something on one of the curtains near the deck door. I looked up and saw a bird. "Kathy, come quick!" I looked around and saw another feathered creature on the Christmas tree. Kathy followed with a "What in the world?" I eased toward the bird on the curtain. It did not move. It was a fake. So was the one on the tree and the third we would find later in the home. It seems the devious Zac and his mom; the daughter of Mr. Beam that we will call Karen had been up to no good. They just loved hearing about our bird shenanigans of the evening before and they thought they would just keep the good times rolling. They had snuck into the home in the middle of the day and planted the fake, feathered friends just for our continued Holiday enjoyment.

Just wait Zac, I drew your name for Christmas!

THE BEST, BEST MAN

Hannah joined the Henderson family 24 years to the date after she joined the Rainey clan. It was June 8th, 2013, a beautiful sunny day at the Lake Guntersville State Park Lodge. The view from the deck of the Lodge is simply fabulous. I mentioned in another writing that the most beautiful sunsets I have ever witnessed are on the island of Maui, Hawaii, but later this particular evening God showed us his artistic work Alabama style. The Lodge from a mountaintop location overlooks Lake Guntersville and its small islands that turn to interesting shaped splotches protruding out of the water as the day ends. The lights from boats some, green, some red and some white send streaks on the water canvas as they make their way into shore for the evening. First the fabulous blue, then yellow, orange, pink and mostly black take their turns coloring the sky in an orderly fashion as the day turns to night. That, however, would come later. At this point in the day, before the afternoon start time of the nuptials, I was witnessing the majesty of two bald eagles flying high above, soaring effortlessly in the bright blue sky.

I felt a moment of introspection as I thought of my parents who had passed within six months of each other in the previous year. To me, the eagles represented mom and dad smiling down from their new heavenly home. My dad had a great relationship with Gabe. I remember the night he first met Hannah at a family gathering at our home. He pulled Gabe aside and with all seriousness looked at him and said: "she's a keeper." That was his way of telling Gabe to be smart and don't lose her. Kathy and I thought how Gabe had the good fortune of needing to remember just one big date each year to stay in the good graces of his bride, June 8th her birthday and their anniversary. Of course, pastor Joey officiated the ceremony and even I had to admit he did a very nice job. That guy makes it hard on this non-pastor, tennis playing, realtor.

Kathy as the mother of the groom chose to wear a beautiful, knee-length, dark blue dress. It had lace that extended just below the knee, covering a little of the calf. It was the perfect color to help camouflage the different hues of blue and purple bruising running down her leg from the hamstring tear she had suffered in a recent tennis match. Kathy was determined to not allow the injury to take away from the festivities. She reminded me with a squeeze of the arm to slow down as we strolled down the aisle during the processional. Although the leg was quite sore and stiff, Kathy managed to make it through the service without the slightest limp.

Alex would serve as the best man. He had his hands full keeping the college and high school friends that were serving as groomsmen in line while making sure Gabe got to the right spot at the right time. He also helped give Gabe all the confidence a new husband should have. There was a last moment scare when Alex hurriedly found the missing mixing sand that had been left in a closet in the Lodge. He found the sand, placed it in the right spot and took off to be with Gabe just seconds before the processional music started. The pink and blue sand would later illustrate the symbolism of Gabe and Hannah as individuals coming together to be one. The sand once mixed cannot be separated and returned to its previous form.

The reception featured a sit-down meal. I got to perform a toast. It was heartfelt and I meant what I said about how Hannah makes Gabe an even better man, but overall it was not an award-winning oration. Now it was the time for Alex to deliver the best man's toast. Alex is gifted in a lot of ways, but his ability to spin a yarn or present architectural projects to a room full of executives is just entertaining.

I once saw a park project presentation that he delivered to family and friends at Lion's Park in Greensboro, Alabama as a part of the Auburn University Rural Studio program. There were a lot of things to see that day and time was precious. Alex had a few hundred folks smiling while humming Gypsy by Fleetwood Mac. This was being played as Alex ran in place and explained the virtues of the park improvements. The video was on fast-forward as Alex whizzed past the walking trail patrons on the screen. His quick pace helped make sure the day's events stayed on schedule. He has a way of being creative and pulling out the fun in a project but keeping the perspective of what is trying to be accomplished.

A couple of years before the wedding, Gabe had purchased a home. It had certainly seen its share of bachelor days as well as a bachelor's decorating touches. Roxy, the rat terrier looking dog that found her way one evening to Gabe's doorstep lived there as well. The neighborhood was great for Gabe. He tried his hand working a small garden in the back. The older neighbors on either side likely shook their heads as he attempted the shortcuts to growing. They knew to do it right required persistence and patience, not a combination easily found in today's twenty-somethings. Gabe was pretty fond of hot peppers and did succeed in creating some tasty and almost nuclear hot habaneros and ghost peppers. Once at a local restaurant, Gabe signed a waiver and tried the hottest chicken wings on the menu. He ate them but paid the price as his whole insides burned from the experience. Thank goodness for the local Mapco/Exxon convenience store less than a block away. Gabe made a couple of trips that evening as he purchased and then consumed milk to try and sooth the burn. That convenience store is also the place of work for Gabe's confidant. I have never met the guy, but Gabe would mention talking to the gentleman about a lot of life's quirks and hear the wisdom from the clerk as he shared his point of view.

I tell that to get back to Alex and the best man's speech. "First", Alex started, "I would like to say to all the bridesmaids, whose dates are the envy of all the single men here, that you all look beautiful and I want to thank you for adding so much to the wedding as Hannah and Gabe spoke their vows. To Hannah, today my brother is the luckiest man alive. He is lucky to have you for his wife and good friends to help him with life's big decisions, help that includes the day he proposed. You see, for those of you who may not know the story, Gabe had purchased the engagement ring and then picked it up early on a Friday. All day it was burning a hole in his pocket, as he wanted to give it to Hannah at the earliest possible moment. He convinced himself to stick with the plan of proposing that night at dinner. Hannah was already at Gabe's house when he excused himself and left the home to pick up something. Truthfully Gabe was a nervous young man. Many of you in this room may have felt a similar way before you asked the big question. Gabe knew this was a step that he wanted to take and that Hannah was the one, but he had to have just one more counseling session from his good friend and advisor. For about fifteen minutes Hannah patiently waited for Gabe while stroking the short hair of Roxy's back. After another thirty minutes, she began to get a little frustrated at Gabe's sudden departure, lack of information as to where he was going and the fact that her stomach was now growling. Gabe was nowhere else but one block away at the Exxon station talking to his advisor of life, the clerk. Now the clerk had met Hannah as she had visited the store with Gabe from time to time, so he had no trouble recommending to Gabe that he should get back to the house and not wait another second. He encouraged Gabe to walk in the door, get down on a knee, pull out the ring and ask the question. "Don't wait around," he said, "get 'er done!" My brother after one more emotional charge from the clerk did just that. Gabe sensing that Hannah would be frustrated with him for leaving her alone did not wait on dinner. He walked in the door, showed the ring and asked the question. So, Hannah, you can see why Gabe is the luckiest man alive because, in spite of all of that, you still said yes. May you two share all the happiness this world can offer." The toast was complete but no one could take a drink for a few seconds. The place was rolling with laughter at the story Alex had told and the picture he had painted of Gabe's afternoon. I was laughing so hard I was crying and Gabe, as is his normal response when embarrassed, picked up the glass of ice water and raised it to his mouth to help cover his blushing face.

The next several minutes were celebratory for many and terrifying for a few. The daddy-daughter dance was sweet as Frank, the former college football lineman and Hannah took over the dance floor. Kathy, with tears glistening in her green eyes bravely and beautifully, danced the mother-son dance.

The hamstring pain seemed momentarily distant. Moms have always been able to find amazing determination when it comes to their children. Gabe now had a family of his own. Wow, how time flies she thought as the tears got just a little heavier and gravity pulled one down the side of her face and onto the dance floor. The cheers from the crowd showed appreciation for all. Now the fear and panic set in. Mr. and Mrs. Beam were under the impression that they would be the next to be asked to dance. They don't dance. I have never even seen Mr. Beam sway to the beat of a pretty good hymn at church. We did not know of their fear until later. For the Beams, it worked out, as they did not have to dance that day. I wish we had thought about a grandparent's dance, not to be mean (well maybe a little mean) but to see how they would dance together.

Alex would be very busy over the next few hours. He worked hard keeping people on the dance floor either by dancing with them or wowing them with his many moves. Kathy even decided to heck with the injury. She joined the guests on the dance floor and had a great time. She did not fall, pull another muscle or reinjure the hamstring, which was great. The biggest challenge Alex faced would turn out to be keeping all the groomsmen who had been celebrating the occasion with gusto from fighting each other, guests at the hotel, or wrestling the stuffed bear in the hallway. Who knows he may also have compromising photos of one of Gabe's college buddies that vows to be a congressman in the future. You never know when that might come in handy. Gabe chose wisely for his best man as Alex proved to be a great orator, an amazing dancer, a peacemaker, a special brother and the very best, best man.

HANNAH'S NEW HOME

Hannah had her work cut out for her to turn the place into a home that they both could enjoy. They would begin the renovation in the fall of 2013 and for ten weeks would live with us in the home where Gabe had grown up. The residence on the north side of Albertville borders Short Creek, which is actually a small river. Our home was on a ninety-foot bluff overlooking the creek. Trees, rocks, wildflowers, oak-leaf hydrangeas and yes briars dotted the scenery from the back deck all the way to the water. All kinds of critters lived in the woods. We would see the occasional opossum, skunk, fox, beaver, and rabbit, just about anything that could squeeze into a hole or make a den in the rocks. Of course, squirrels are abundant as are birds, featuring tons of woodpeckers. I did learn some interesting things during those weeks together. One was that Hannah liked oatmeal with cinnamon for breakfast and another was that she had a sharp wit about her that enabled her to stand toe to toe with Gabe and me. Kathy now had an ally about the house and the two seemed to enjoy putting the guys in their place. Kathy and I found it entertaining to have the duo around the house, but I am sure they were beyond relieved when their kitchen remodeling was completed and they could enjoy setting up their own place.

Fast forward to August of 2014. After many conversations about our housing future, Kathy and I looked at a home in a neighborhood near Mr. and Mrs. Beam and of course Joey and his family. By December we had negotiated a deal. The whole story of the purchase is amazing and I will not go into that here, but just understand, it would have to be the perfect situation and the belief that it was totally God's will for me to leave my Northridge home. I had developed that subdivision and raised my family there. For me, it was a very difficult transition, but God moved in perfect timing for both the owner and for us. He is pretty good at that perfect timing gig.

The transition was made easier when Hannah and Gabe agreed to buy the home of Gabe's childhood, leaving behind the newly transformed, former bachelor pad. We closed on the new home in January of 2015 and after allowing a little time for the owner to move we began a pretty extensive remodel of our own. Fortunately, Gabe and Hannah were in no hurry to move so we stayed at Northridge during the construction.

On February 6th, the birthday of Gabe, Ronald Reagan, and Babe Ruth, I was playing an early morning game of basketball. At some point in the second game, I did a pump fake, took a dribble to my left and jumped to shoot the now open shot. A sound that resonated in my ears like a gun going off and a sudden pain in my lower left leg landed me on my tail as my Achilles tendon ruptured. The guys, as guys do, offered to help me up and asked if I was all right as I limped over to the bleachers to retrieve my warm-up clothing. Then they looked around and said, "Who's in for Greg?" No one walked me to my car or anything, but they were doing the understood thing. That is the way it is in old man sports. If you are going to play in your fifties, something is going to get hurt, so be prepared and there is not much compassion. As I got to my car I realized I had some problems. The obvious one was that my ankle was no longer connected like it used to be to my leg. It kind of dangled and obviously did not react like normal. Another was that for some reason it seemed like a good idea that morning to drive my bright red 2005 BMW Z4 with the black soft top. Of course, it was a six-speed manual transmission. I would now need to navigate the six-mile journey to my office during school hour traffic. I would also be pressing the clutch each time I needed to shift gears with my torn ankle. The first few shifts were quite painful and just not that easy. I vowed I would not go over 45 and that way there would be no need to shift any higher than third gear. Then as it sometimes does in these situations, fate decided to throw me another zinger. I had worked my way in traffic and was now squarely behind a school bus that was stopping every 200 feet to pick up kids eager to expand their intellect. Now, I was shifting more than ever as I had to stop and then start back up. I am not necessarily proud of what I was thinking at this moment because to place my situation in the situation of soldiers is ludicrous, but hear me out. I had been to see the movie Lone Survivor. The courage shown forth in that film is beyond compare. For me, all I kept telling myself was "Hey, you got a little Achilles tear. Those guys in Lone Survivor were falling off cliffs, breaking bones and being shot and they kept going as long as they could. Surely you can finish this drive you little wimp." I talk to myself sometimes like that. I have to get on my own case to keep pushing forward. I finally made it to the office. My original plan had been to shower there and just eat breakfast downtown near my work. Instead, I made that call that husbands hate to make, the call to your wife to tell her that I had been injured trying to hold on to my youth. I must say, Kathy was gracious and compassionate. She just took a sick day and prepared to chauffeur me around for a long day of doctors and decisions. However, looking back she may have had a more opportunistic plan up her pretty little sleeve.

I placed a call to my sister Cindy, the nurse practitioner that worked with the Huntsville Hospital system. She had been with the orthopedic group at one time and knew the doctors. One call from her and I was on a short list of standby patients for that very morning. Huntsville is about forty-five miles from Albertville. Carol Slivka on her way to the administration building of Huntsville Hospital zoomed by us as she hurried to account for all the money coming into and out of the hospital. Her perception at such speed is quite incredible. She later told us that she knew something bad must have happened if I was in the back seat. Over the years both Carol and Cindy have made friends with several of the police and highway patrol personnel that oversee that stretch of highway.

My worst fear was confirmed at the 9:30 doctor's appointment. The Achille's tendon was torn completely in two. The doctor later described it as looking like two pieces of frayed rope. It was decided that surgery would be at 5:00 that very afternoon. I was to have nothing to eat or drink until surgery was complete. Since we were in Huntsville with time to kill and I had been given some crutches, Kathy decided that we should do some shopping for all things home renovation. Did I mention that she might have something up her sleeve? I mean, I admit that I did not want to sit around at the hospital all day, but from my standpoint and psyche, I had just endured an injury that may very well be the end to 42 years of playing tennis. Compassionate Kathy had more pressing things on her mind like, say, looking at appliances, flooring, and oh wait, yes there is a decorator store just over there. Each stop provided a new adventure and adjustment to the use of my new apparatuses for mobilization. Some stores had several steps. Now let me see going up it is crutches first, no foot first, what is it? I would have asked Kathy for some advice but once the doorbell of the store chimed, it was like the gate had opened at the Kentucky Derby and this little filly was running for the roses. By the time I had teetered over to the hardwood aisle of store number one, she had managed to pull out four choices of various shades of planks to study over and peruse. The next stop would be appliances. I quickly discovered that tile floors were even more of a challenge. I then heard the words, "hey, doesn't that dishwasher look nice." I quickly pointed out that Kathy is indeed the nicest looking dishwasher that I have ever seen.

A few minutes later I was still rubbing my shoulder. As lunchtime approached, Kathy headed toward the Jones Valley set of stores and a favorite Asian restaurant. I decided that since I could not eat that I would just sit in the back seat and wait for her to finish the meal. If you have never just sat in a car in a crowded parking lot, you should try it. It can provide some entertaining moments. You would be amazed at the near misses of doors, buggies, and vehicles as people enter and exit their cars and parking spots. There is also a whole lot of discarded chewing gum, cigarette butts and other semi biodegradable items tossed about for our viewing pleasure. When Kathy ventured back she had a "to go" cup filled with some liquid to wash down the buckwheat noodles and a satisfied smile on her face. I could just sit and think that in another eight hours that could be me. We then journeyed through Target and Barnes and Noble before heading back toward the hospital. "What just happened," I asked myself as I realized I had just spent about five hours shopping for home remodeling items.

There is never a good time for an injury like this and certainly, it was unfortunate timing for me as well. The Aggie tennis team was beginning to get ready for the season. I would spend the next few months trying to coach from crutches that would occasionally get stuck in the mud of the often wet spring grass surrounding our courts. Kathy was awesome as she patiently helped me through the struggles. By June the renovations were complete and it was moving time for not only Kathy and me but for Gabe and Hannah. With the help of a local moving company, we were both in our new homes.

Hannah, as mentioned earlier, had experienced ten weeks of living at Northridge in the mid to late fall but had not had the spring perspicacity. Being excited about the new place, she and Gabe invited her parents and relatives over for Sunday lunch. After lunch, Hannah's mother Bonnie and nephew Jace were looking from the deck over the bluff and toward the water. The big black stick on a fallen tree, some sixty feet below particularly enamored them. As others joined them on the deck the black stick slithered away causing several shrieks from the guests. Gabe had grown up around them and laughed, but Hannah filed away the fact that a big snake might live nearby. Her uncle, a country guy as well, got a big laugh out of it and joked with Hannah about the snake coming to get her. Another thing that had happened that spring and in others previously was that birds had built their nests in the corners of the carport. Now to each his own when deciding to allow birds to nest in their porch. I just always hated the thoughts of removing the nest until after the baby birds had left home. In just a few days the nest would be empty. The hatchlings were growing strong.

The next day, Monday afternoon as Hannah got out of her car in the carport after a hard day's work, she saw something next to the steps leading into the home. Startled for a moment she quickly got her wits about her as she surmised that her Uncle had pulled the old rubber snake trick on her. As she approached the steps and fiddled with her key chain looking for the key to unlock the door, she caught a glimpse of a slight movement. Her focus shifted from the keys to the reptile as she began to realize that it was not a sinister uncle's joke but a live king snake. Suddenly, Hannah pulled a Superman stunt and leaped the four steps to the door in a single bound. Once inside she quickly sent a text to her favorite father-in-law thanking me for selling her a snake-infested home. I just let her know it was all part of the ambiance. I thought I was pretty funny until a few moments later she sent a photo along with a little more frantic text. The photo showed that the snake had moved from next to the door and had made its way up the column of the carport wrapping itself securely as it scaled the height to reach a small ledge where the birds nest was built and the proud parents had hatched their young. The photo showed one of the hatchlings halfway inside the predator's mouth. I really was saddened by the image and I felt sorry for the cautiously courageous Hannah. It was hard to imagine how a first week could start tougher than Hannah's first three days at her new home, but Tuesday morning took it to another level.

It started normally. Gabe left for work at the bank and Hannah hopped into the shower to get ready for a day of accounting. As she turned off the water she heard the dogs whining to go outside. She donned some shorts and a t-shirt, opened the door to the once snake inhabited carport and stepped outside with Roxy and Riley. Being new to the dwelling, she was not experienced with all the intricacies, like how the doors automatically lock when you close them unless you release the latch on the knob, which she failed to do. Moments later a bit of panic set in as Hannah without success attempted to open first the carport door, then the front and deck doors. All were locked. "Where is my cell phone?" inquisitive Hannah asked herself only to have realistic Hannah say, "Inside, where you left it." She argued with herself about breaking a window or not and then

142

decided against it. So there she was, wet hair, no shoes and clothed like a bra-burning women's libber. She decided to start the journey, hoping to find a neighbor that would answer the door of an early morning knock. She looked and saw a pair of Gabe's old tennis shoes and she put them on. Now Hannah has some pretty big feet. They are not wide, but long and narrow, Gabe however, wears a size 12. I wish that I had thought to go to the video recorder of the outdoor cameras at their home and saved the video, but I did not think of it. Hannah started up the 200-foot driveway with Roxy and Riley nipping at the flopping shoes covering her feet. She decided to try the house across the street and made her way up the steps to knock on the door. Imagine the surprise of Mr. McGriff the homeowner when he first set eyes on the new neighbor that looked like she had just stepped out of Woodstock after the rain-soaked Ravi Shankar opening evening musical set. Suppressing any outward laughter, he graciously allowed Hannah to use his telephone to call Gabe to come and open the locked home.

Sore shoulders are a trait of Henderson men and Gabe had to massage his after the closed fist struck him for doubling over with laughter at seeing his bride sitting on the carport steps with the two dogs vying for her attention. A couple of moments after settling back inside the home, Roxy snuggled up to Hannah. A short time afterward Hannah let out a scream as she saw a tick crawling on her pet. Move me back to town could be heard throughout the neighborhood as she opened the door and tossed the small arachnid back into the wild.

EPILOGUE

Since the writing of The Amazing Mr. Beam and through the completion of this book our family has maintained reasonably good health. Cassie and Kaden have had a son, Dawson to go along with daughter Kinlie Jo, now almost starting school. Hannah and Gabe are expecting a daughter in the coming months. This will give the Beams four great-grandchildren. Alex is living in North Carolina outside of Asheville where he and several others are creating a craft school called The Cabbage School. Alex is in charge of some design-build classes. The main person at the school is Jessica Green. Jessica is a world-renowned weaver of goods. She owns the land, raises and shears the sheep, dyes and then produces the product. Alex also continues to write and produce his music. He just completed a twelve-song tract that he is hoping to soon share with the world. When the school is not is session he travels and completes design-build projects all over the place. Many times he works with Coco, a young lady that he seems to be quite fond of. She owns a tea business and is quite an accomplished craftsman as well. Gabe is about a week away from leaving the banking world and joining me in the real estate business. I am looking forward to having him on board. Gabe is also a certified tennis instructor. Hannah is a CPA with a local firm and is as quick-witted as ever. She is a great mom and one of the few people that can get away with calling me, Gregory. Gamble just turned three and is a delight. Time flies, but it is sure fun to watch him grow. My sister Cindy and her husband Mike are now grandparents as their son Michael and his wife Emily now have a son named Wyatt. Cindy is still running a medical clinic in Huntsville and Mike is mostly retired but has a business of enhancing motorcycles with specialty kits. Their other son Allen is a very busy attorney in Albertville. He helps me with some real estate opportunities from time to time.

Tommy Winkles and Ann live in Murfreesboro, Tennessee. He is a great family man and still a whole bunch of fun. The rumor is also floating around that he may try to recapture a particular moment in time at his upcoming fiftieth high school reunion. Yikes! All I am saying about this is that Gil Bruce now lives in Carrollton, Georgia. All of you with a fear of mayonnaise may want to check out Albertville as a place to call home. I could not move for a month or so, but it was for a great cause. Gil and his wife Sherry spend a lot of time working with autism awareness. Their daughter Kelly was diagnosed with the disorder early in her childhood, but with love, care and the support of a great school system, she graduated high school as a classmate of Alex. John and Carol Slivka are soon to be grandparents, so exciting times await them as well. Joey is still pastor of Solitude Baptist Church and the church is still growing. Karen does a fantastic job as a pastor's wife. That is a tough role. Can you imagine if the preacher has a bad day delivering the Sunday message being the person that has to critique the work and still give him a shot of confidence for the next time? It takes a team to pastor a church and they are a great team. Zac seems to blow out more motors on his wheelchair than a NASCAR team does in a year. He still loves the Atlanta Braves and the Alabama Crimson Tide. He just turned thirty-three.

As I conclude, I just want to say again that I am a man most blessed. I have at this point decent health, amazing friends and a wonderful family. I love my work and the town that I call home. I truly believe that my joy stems from my relationship with God and having accepted his son Jesus as my lord and savior. In this time in our nation's history, I say do not listen to all the noise around you, but experience for yourself what comfort a Christian life can bring. I wish for you, joy and peace.

God Bless!

EPILOGUE #2

After the completion of this book, during the editing and before production, we lost the Amazing Mr. Beam. It happened suddenly after he spent a beautiful Saturday enjoying his yard and his family. In the early evening hours as he was sitting in his favorite chair, God called him home. The enormous support of prayers, visits and cards from people that knew and loved him, strengthened all the family. He is greatly missed, but our family faith is strong and our hearts full of peace as we know that he is in the presence of our Heavenly Father.

IN LOVING MEMORY

Paul Jerry Beam

August 27, 1939-May 12, 2019

For your Christian love, great smile, infectious laugh, family values and teaching me how to stop, smell and enjoy the flowers along this life's journey, I thank you Mr. Beam……………I mean dad.

www.ingramcontent.com/pod-product-compliance
Lightning Source LLC
Chambersburg PA
CBHW050132280326
41933CB00010B/1351